Fire in Coventry

Stephen Verney

A new edition introduced
by Christopher Cocksworth,
Bishop of Coventry

The Diocese of Coventry

© Stephen Verney 1964

First published in 1964
in Great Britain by
Hodder and Stoughton Ltd,
London

Abbreviated and revised
edition published in 1996
in the USA by
Austin Publishing Co,
Atlanta, Georgia

Scripture quotations are from the
Authorised King James Version or
the New English Bible

A new edition introduced
by Christopher Cocksworth,
Bishop of Coventry 2010

Introduction © Christopher Cocksworth 2010

Scripture quotations are from the
New Revised Standard Version of the Bible

Published by
The Diocese of Coventry,
1 Hill Top, Coventry, CV1 5AB
www.coventry.anglican.org

ISBN: 978-0-9565607-0-4

Typeset in Gill Sans and Coventry
Design and typesetting by Jon Ashby
www.jonasdesign.co.uk

Printed and bound by Print5, Coventry

Editorial and typographical note

This 2010 edition is published in the lead-up to Coventry Cathedral's Golden Jubilee in 2012, the 50th Anniversary of the consecration of the new Cathedral.

The new edition allows Stephen Verney's 1964 text to speak for itself. No attempt has been made to update or revise the content. However, some linguistic changes have been made where idiom has altered and the original vocabulary might hinder communication of the author's meaning. In particular, most generic uses of masculine nouns and pronouns have been removed, where the author is not quoting other sources, and the practice, now gaining acceptance, of using the singular 'they/their/them' has been employed.

The 'Coventry' typeface, based on Ralph Beyer's lettering on the Tablets of the Word, has been used for the quotations facing pages 18, 23, 89 and 141 and on the back cover. The quotations, which have been added to this edition, facing pages 89 and 141, are taken from two of the Tablets of the Word on the walls of the new Cathedral.

Contents

Introduction to the 2010 edition

by **Christopher Cocksworth,**
Bishop of Coventry

I first came across this 'small book whose importance is out of all proportion to its size' (as Donald Coggan, one-time Archbishop of Canterbury, described it[1]) shortly after it became known that I was to be the next Bishop of Coventry. It arrived as a gift from one of Cambridge University's Divinity Professors who had been confirmed by Cuthbert Bardsley, one of my most notable predecessors and the writer of the powerful Foreword to the first edition that you will find in a few pages' time. In an accompanying letter my professor friend told me that the book tells the story of a revival of spiritual life in the Diocese of Coventry, a revival that he hoped might happen again in some new form in the future. This was more than enough to set me to the task of reading it. Actually, I devoured it. I was convinced that I was reading much more than a story of a remarkable period in the life of one diocese in the Church of England. I felt I was handling a spiritual classic relevant to every age and all the churches – truly, as Stephen Verney wrote in his Introduction, 'a book about the Holy Spirit'. I wanted to get it back out into the life of the Church and I wanted to start with each minister of the gospel in the Diocese of Coventry in the hope that, like the story of which it speaks, its message would gradually ripple outwards embracing more and more people.

When I arrived in the diocese in the latter part of 2008 I was delighted to discover that Stephen Verney was still alive, though by now very frail. We spoke together on the telephone and I was able to hear more about the story of *Fire in Coventry* from the author himself. Stephen graciously agreed to be interviewed by my assistant James Hill and excerpts of the interview, where Stephen movingly reflects on the deep themes of the book, can be found on the diocesan website.[2] Sadly, Stephen died in 2009 but not before giving his permission for the book to be republished. I am extremely grateful not only to Stephen for his generosity but also to Sandra, his widow, who has been enormously supportive throughout the process.

Although by 2008 *Fire in Coventry* was a fairly faint memory in the diocese, a number of people independently expressed interest in its republication, including the Friends of Coventry Cathedral and among them Margaret Lloyd in particular, about whom I will say more at the end of this Introduction. Nevertheless, the moment of truth came when a decision needed to be made about whether to take the plunge and go ahead with a new edition. It was not only financial considerations that had to be taken into account. There were more fundamental, more spiritual, questions. Would this story from the past help take the Diocese of Coventry – and any other readers – into the future to which God was calling us? Or would it be a distraction from what the book so discerningly asks: 'what in particular, O Lord God who created the universe, do you want *us* to do *now?*' (p.31). Even worse, would it be a bit of indulgent reminiscence that would romanticise the past and make us wish that we could return to those glorious days when the eyes of the world seemed to be upon Coventry as its bombed Cathedral arose from the ruins as a symbol of post-war British confidence, political and ecclesiastical?

I was given good advice. 'Bishop, go away and read it again, and if *Fire in Coventry* still lights a fire of hope about what God might do among us now, then we should publish it again without hesitation.' I did as I was told and read the book again while on a Lenten retreat. It had the same effect, though even more so now that I knew the names of the places it describes and could imagine, for example, the Coventry Cross of Nails being passed on from parish to parish across the length and breadth of this very special diocese right in the heart of England. To quote Donald Coggan again, 'that the Spirit of God was at work' in the events that the book describes, 'there could be no doubt'.[3] For that reason alone, the book deserves to be accessible again. But it is much more than a record of the past. It is a story of permanent relevance because it uncovers some of the deepest characteristics of the life of the Church and of the great mystery of divine and human interplay as God breaks into the affairs of the world with a particular intensity. I would like to draw attention to three of the main themes of *Fire in Coventry* – Love, Prayer and the Holy Spirit and then to make a few comments on what the book says about the nature of a diocese.

The first part of *Fire in Coventry* tells the story of the lead-up to the consecration of the new Cathedral in 1962. The second reflects on what God was doing throughout the diocese during this period. Both parts end with a sort of meditation on Love, Prayer and the Holy Spirit, picturing them as dancers 'at the heart of the Church' (p.85) where 'first one, then another, holds the centre of the stage; they hold hands and dance together; they weave in and out and through one another in intricate patterns' (p.136). Stephen Verney is reluctant to try to put the dancers in any definitive order for fear of turning the adventure of faith into a transaction of religion. As if it were a case of saying, '*if* we love, *then* we will pray, *then* the Spirit will come'; or, '*if* we are open to the Spirit, *then* we will love, *then* we will pray'. The intricate patterns woven by the intimate interplay between God's action and our response are much more subtle and interesting, much more *grace laden*, than our attempts to work out laws of Christian living. Nevertheless, I would like to explore this 'dance at the heart of the Church' by beginning with the work of the Holy Spirit breaking open a readiness to respond to the calling of God in the Diocese of Coventry during those years.

Perhaps it was the legacy of the bombing of the city and Cathedral in 1940 that created a Church culture that knew that even the greatest accomplishments of the human spirit can be demolished – literally – overnight. Perhaps it was to do not only with the physical and financial enormity of building a Cathedral in the middle of the twentieth century, but also the spiritual and moral responsibility to shape a sign of the future required by a world structured for peace. Perhaps it was the sort of people God was gathering to serve and lead the diocese at that time. Whatever the cause, there seems to have been in the diocese that 'moment', which Stephen Verney describes, 'of helplessness and humility in which we are ready to accept God's gift' (p.105). This is the beginning of spiritual life as the Christian gospel understands it. The point where we accept, in the words of the Anglican collect, that 'we have no power of ourselves to help ourselves'. It is the heartfelt prayer of blind Bartimaeus who calls out to Jesus, 'Have mercy on me' (Mark 10:46). It is the basic principle of Church life – that we are entirely dependent on the presence and power of the Holy Spirit and that we need, what the eighteenth-century Anglican Divine, William Law, called, 'the perpetual inspiration of the Holy Spirit'.

Cuthbert Bardsley was very conscious of the challenges and opportunities facing the Church in the 1960s. Fifty years on those challenges have grown enormously. The place of Christian faith in our society has diminished considerably and the resources of the Church along with it. Yet, in the same proportion, the opportunities before us are huge as much of Britain becomes once more a primary mission field. Our greatest challenge and our greatest opportunity is to reach that same point now, as they did then, and to cry out the prayer with which this book begins:

Come, Holy Spirit,
fill the hearts of thy faithful people,
and kindle in us the fire of thy love.

This beautiful prayer proves Stephen Verney's point about the 'dance at the heart of the Church' and the interplay between the Holy Spirit, Love and Prayer. Clearly the Holy Spirit was calling the diocese to a deeper level of prayer in those days. Beginning with the fundamental prayer for the energising strength of the Holy Spirit, many people found themselves seeking God's will, not only for direction, but also for the detail of what obeying God's will at that time and that place involved. Their prayer was what *in particular* the creator of heaven and earth was calling them to be and to do. They were ready to take time to ask and to listen to what the *Spirit was saying to the churches* and they did so together, not just individually. What I find so interesting is that when the first sense of a stirring of the Spirit in the Monks Kirby Chapter was reported back to the Bishop, he did not immediately act on it but waited to see whether others in different parts of the diocese were hearing the same voice. When it was becoming clear that they were, Cuthbert, together with the team that formed around him, began to develop a staged strategy to respond to what God seemed to be saying, each step soaked in prayer.

The more I travel around the Diocese of Coventry today, the more I realise the absolute necessity of prayer to our life together and to all that God is wanting to do among and through us. This is true on at least three levels. First there is the prayer of which we have already spoken – the recognition before God of our utter dependence upon God. This leads into a disciplined listening for the word of God for us today, so that we can be the *particular* people and do the *particular* work that God has prepared for us in our time and place. This process of prayer for guidance is necessarily corporate. It is a shared task of discerning where God is leading his people, of learning to hear how the Spirit wants to move the body.

The humble prayer of listening and discernment is followed by the obedient prayer of application and action. As Stephen Verney says, 'there is nothing more dangerous than to hear the word of God and not to do it' (p.32). There comes a time when, having discerned God's will, we are entrusted with the responsibility to apply it through our prayer and enact it by our prayer-supported action. I have to admit that there have been times in the past when I have been somewhat cautious about the place of intercessory prayer in the work of God. I have been so committed to the sovereignty of God – God's power over all things – that I have underplayed the part that our prayer, feeble as it is, plays in his purposes. I have not wanted to constrain divine freedom by the vacillation of human prayer. What I have come to recognise more and more, though, is that God *freely chooses* to work out his sovereign purposes through the prayer of his people. This remarkable act of grace, in which God embraces us as co-workers of the new creation, is no better stated than by one of the greatest theologians of the twentieth century, Karl Barth, whose whole theological endeavour was about preserving the freedom, sovereignty and grace of God. In his massive *Church Dogmatics* Barth wrote that:

> concealed within the creaturely movement [of prayer], yet none the less really, there moves the finger and hand and sceptre of the God who rules the world. And what is more, there moves the heart of God, and He Himself is there in all the fullness of His love and wisdom and power.[4]

Behind the prayer of utter dependence and the prayer of disciplined listening and the prayer of obedient intercession, lies the prayer for spiritual renewal. Whether in the heady work of Christian living when exciting things of God are happening around us and there is much to do, or in the drier times when the going is tough and the results are few, it is all too easy to neglect what Stephen Verney calls that which 'matters most of all' (p.93). This is nothing less than 'the one needful thing', the 'better part', which Jesus said that Mary had chosen – to sit at his feet and to enjoy his presence (Luke 10:42). Renewal in the life of the Spirit is the only way by which we will become the sort of 'infectious Christians' (p.56) which this book describes and which, as human history has shown, is an unstoppable force for good in our world.

Brother Ramon, a charismatic Franciscan friar, who was a good friend of Simon Barrington-Ward, successor but one to Cuthbert as Bishop of Coventry, described prayer as 'simply the relationship of the believer in love with the Lord'.[5] We love because God first loved us (1 John 4:19). We turn to God in prayer because there is something deep down in us that knows God is love and that we have been loved into being by God. We seek and pray for God's purposes for the world through the Church because we know that God's will is the will of love, and that God's rule is the rule of love. As we spend time in prayer to the God of love we find that our love for God and our love of all that God loves expands. We discover the truth of Paul's words that 'God's love has been poured into our hearts through the Holy Spirit that has been given to us' (Romans 5:5).

All this was certainly happening in the Diocese of Coventry during the years that *Fire in Coventry* describes. The call to prayer was accompanied by a call to love, and the call to love was worked out in a commitment to meet together for prayer, both in the small groups, which multiplied across the diocese, and around the Cross of Nails as it travelled from parish to parish drawing people into a deep and intensive experience of prayer. It resulted in a genuine experience of the diocese being, as Stephen Verney repeatedly describes it, 'a fellowship of the Holy Spirit' (p.123). It also led to the profound understanding of the Christian way as our calling both 'to *be* the thing which we proclaim' and to 'tell the secret' of love in Jesus Christ (pp.118–120).

Nothing has fundamentally changed in the intervening decades; neither has the need of the world for love nor the core of the Christian gospel altered since Jesus proclaimed the love of God in his teaching, embodied it in his life and demonstrated it in his death. We are as much in need now of the 'miracles of love' of which Cuthbert wrote in his Foreword as were our predecessors then. But perhaps the damage done by the deficit of love is clearer now than in some periods of the nation's history. Our earth suffers the neglect of love and ecological crisis threatens. Our children suffer the breakdown of inherited channels of love as family life is reconstructed on poor foundations with flimsy materials. The moral fabric of our land frays as its binding by the boundaries of love is removed. Our political and economic systems falter and fail as their bearings from the kingdom of love become fainter. The psychological well-being of our people deteriorates, as the price they pay for independence from the source of love is revealed as a destabilising disenchantment with life itself.

Christ's people are to rejoice in the giver of love through worship inspired by his Spirit of love. We are called to tell love's secret in the great story of love in Jesus Christ that unfolds through the pages of scripture, ready to make disciples of those we meet along the way. We are to show that the story of love continues in our common life together as Christ's people and to beware of any lessening of that witness through inattention to love in the Church and the divisions caused by the neglect of committed loving in the household of God. We are to express this love in sacrificial service to our world, seeking to transform the communities of which we are part, locally and globally. We are to call out to the God of love, as generations have before us, praying:

> Lord, you have taught us
> that all our doings without love are nothing worth:
> send your Holy Spirit
> and pour into our hearts that most excellent gift of love,
> the true bond of peace and of all virtues,
> without which whoever lives is counted dead before you.
> Grant this for your only Son Jesus Christ's sake,
> who is alive and reigns with you,
> in the unity of the Holy Spirit,
> one God, now and for ever.

Now for some words about the nature of a diocese that I think we – especially here in the Diocese of Coventry – can learn from this little book 'whose importance is out of all proportion to its size'. And in these reflections I apologise to readers from further afield for whom the whole concept of a diocese, let alone one particular diocese in England, is remote. I can only hope that you will jump straight into the text itself or find something in the next paragraphs that you can apply to the structures of your own Church.

The work of God described in *Fire in Coventry* helped the people of the Diocese of Coventry to see that a diocese is not meant to be an administrative system or a loose network of parishes. It is to be a living expression of the Church: 'a body alive with a spirit' (p.61), as Stephen Verney beautifully describes it. Here we have an authentic embodiment of the universal Church in a body that comprises a number of interdependent communities of faith bound together in a common life of worship, witness and service, and gathered around a Bishop whose ordination physically connects them with other manifestations of the Church, catholic and apostolic. A diocese, as they discovered then, is not an ecclesiastical device to manage the Church but 'a missionary force' to change the world. None of this is to lessen the role of the parish, benefice and other rooted communities throughout this or any other diocese which remain the Church's front line missionary units. Like any healthy body, our diocese is at its strongest when each parish becomes 'more truly itself' (p.52) and when individual communities are supporting each other in the process. They are to be supported and nourished by the central organs of the diocese which are there to serve the mission of the Church in the particular places and networks across the Church. The interdependence of parishes and communities may explain why *Fire in Coventry* suggests that the deanery 'may be one of the keys to the revival of church life' (p.126). The Diocese of Coventry in the present is taking up this hint from the diocese in the past. We are exploring ways in which the local Dean can be a strategic missionary leader and the Deanery an effective missionary force in a given area of the diocese.

Bodies are continually changing in order to remain alive. The same is true for the Church and for the body of this or any other diocese. The missionary demands before us in the twenty-first century will require energy and agility. We will need to adapt to our changing environment, attentive to the leading of the Spirit who calls us to be faithful to Christ in our own generation. We will need what I have called elsewhere 'ecclesial imagination'[6] as we take our part in what Stephen Verney calls 'a rebirth of the full catholic tradition in contemporary form' (p.125).

When people are made Bishops in the Church of England they are given a Charge by their Archbishop. The Archbishop of Canterbury, Rowan Williams, successor to Augustine who re-evangelised so much of the land, began mine by saying, 'release the missionary energies of the Diocese of Coventry'. This is what happened in the lead-up to the consecration of the new Cathedral in 1962 when God moved his people to open the 'sluice gates' (p.121) of the Spirit and set free the life and love of the good news of Jesus Christ. Pray God that the same may happen in our day.

The republication of this book has relied on the support, hard work and generosity of many. I have already mentioned Stephen and Sandra Verney without whom, of course, nothing would have happened. Margaret Lloyd has also been mentioned but much more should be said than space allows. Her initial vision for the project and her skilful work in bringing it to fruition have been vital to its success. I am also most grateful to David Hollway and John Lloyd for retyping the original text, to Jon Ashby for his cover design and typesetting, and to Amanda Kay for her proofreading. Matt Jermyn has played an important part in publicising the book and Simon Lloyd has been, as ever, readily supportive of a gleam in a Bishop's eye! Finally, I would like to record my great thanks to Christine Camfield, Maureen Prett and especially to James Hill who has lived with the republication of *Fire in Coventry* from the earliest stages and seen it through to the end.

Christopher Coventry

1   D. Coggan, *Cuthbert Bardsley: Bishop, Evangelist, Pastor* (London: Collins, 1989) p.154.
2   http://www.coventry.anglican.org
3   Coggan, *Cuthbert Bardsley*, p.156.
4   K. Barth, *Church Dogmatics*, vol. III/3, eds. Geoffrey W. Bromiley, Thomas Forsyth Torrance (Edinburgh: T. & T. Clark, 1960) p.288.
5   Br. Ramon, *Flame of Sacred Love*, (Abingdon: The Bible Reading Fellowship, 1999) pp.51–2.
6   C. J. Cocksworth, *Holding Together: Gospel, Church and Spirit* (Norwich: Canterbury Press, 2008).

+

THEN THE FIRE
OF THE LORD FELL

I Kings 18:38

Foreword
to the 1964 edition

From Cuthbert Bardsley,
Bishop of Coventry 1956–1976

This is a story of experience – the events in this book took place in the Diocese of Coventry, but most of them could have taken place, and in many cases have taken place, in other dioceses. It is far from being a 'success story', for we have learned as much through failure as through success – nevertheless, the events are recorded in this book in the hope that they may bring encouragement to tired and frustrated clergy and laity.

We live in difficult days, when the foundations of our faith are being questioned and when age-old moral laws are being disregarded. At such a moment it is good to be reminded that the Holy Spirit is still mightily at work; that when man listens, God still speaks; that when man obeys, God still works his miracles of love.

This book has been written in the spirit of prayer and is the work of a man of prayer. It is my hope that it will be read prayerfully, with time for quiet meditation at the end of each chapter. Let us pray together that we Churchmen may rise to the opportunities of this hour, not wallowing in self-pity, nor basking in self-satisfaction, but humbly, penitently and with an obedient heart, place ourselves unreservedly at the disposal of the Holy Spirit, so that under his leadership we may discover the lessons that he would have us learn and bear our witness effectively to this bewildered, frustrated and rootless generation.

Cuthbert Coventry

COME
HOLY SPIRIT
+ FILL THE HEARTS OF
THY FAITHFUL PEOPLE
AND KINDLE IN US
THE FIRE OF
THY LOVE

Introduction

In the winter of 1940 the city of Coventry was blitzed and the Cathedral destroyed by fire. Twenty-one years later, in the summer of 1962, amongst the millions of visitors from all over the world who crowded into Coventry to visit the new Cathedral, came a husband and wife – he was by origin a German Jew, a refugee from Hitler and she a Greek, and they had made their home in South Africa.

After they had looked round the Cathedral and taken part in a short service they sat for a time in silence. Then the wife said, 'I'm sorry, I can't speak.' After another silence she said, 'If only it were true!' and burst into tears.

Like many other visitors they found themselves confronted not just by a modern cathedral and by contemporary works of art – there was something more. They felt like travellers in a dry land who stumble upon water. They caught a glimpse of happiness, and of the human race united round the living Jesus. 'If only it were true!' Or was it a mirage?

This book sets out to show that it was true and to describe what it was that they had stumbled upon. It is a book about the Holy Spirit. It is written by an ordinary person for ordinary people, and it contains no long theological words. But it attempts, with a certain sense of awe and gratitude, to tell what God said and did in the Coventry Diocese as we prepared for the consecration of the new Cathedral.

This is an exciting time to be a Christian because after a period of disillusion we can hear God speaking to the Church all over the world and showing us the way forward. What he has said here in Coventry, he is saying everywhere, only the message seems to have been given to us with extraordinary simplicity and in a dramatic form which is easily understood. It has been more than a message – we have actually experienced the power and the love of God taking hold of us. This book is an 'honest to God' attempt to make an accurate report of what actually happened, and if it has at all succeeded then perhaps it may help to throw some light upon what God himself thinks about the *Honest to God* controversy.

An old soldier said to me the other day that Field Marshal Montgomery's description of a battle bears little resemblance to what actually took place. There are in fact two ways of reporting a battle, either as it appears to the commander-in-chief, who sees it as a whole, or as it appears to a soldier in the thick of the fighting. I am in the lucky position of being able to report this campaign from both points of view. As a parish priest I was personally embroiled in everything here described, but at the same time I am Diocesan Missioner, a kind of staff-officer to the Bishop who is our commander-in-chief. I hope, therefore, that the details of the story will ring true to the soldiers, but that at the same time the book as a whole will reveal God's general strategy; for what he has said and done can only be fully grasped as reports come in from all corners of the diocese. It is part of his plan that we should only be able to understand *together*.

Part One of the book is based on these reports. It is a description of *what actually happened* and it uses as far as possible words written or spoken at the time. When Part One was finished, I read it through and noted down sixty-three significant points which seemed to arise from the story. These sixty-three points form the basis of Part Two, which is an attempt to draw out the *meaning of what happened*. By this method I have tried to let the events speak for themselves and reveal to us what God has said and done – but inevitably my own limitations will have distorted the truth, and for that I apologise to all who shared these experiences with me.

One thing must be emphasised above all else, that *this is not a success story*. It is something that happened to us and most of the time seemed to be happening in spite of us. We made every kind of mistake. We tried to impose our own preconceived ideas. We grumbled and doubted. If I have emphasised the successful side of the story, it is because the success was God's and because I am convinced that his strength has been made perfect in our weakness, to speak words of encouragement to the Church.

This book is dedicated to all those who have helped me to write it by showing me the meaning of Love, Prayer and Reality: especially to my friends and neighbours in the parish of Leamington Hastings and most particularly to my wife.

---

1   John A. Robinson, *Honest to God*, 1963.

Part One

The Story

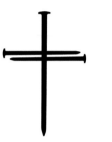

Chapter 1

Monks Kirby

A group of clergy were meeting in a suburb of Coventry and to understand what follows you must understand first who those clergy were.

They were called the Monks Kirby Chapter. This sounds rather sinister, but is in fact quite harmless. Church of England parishes are divided into groups called rural deaneries and the clergy of that group are known as a chapter. They meet once a month or so, under their Rural Dean. They receive instructions from the Bishop and they organise joint activities. Sometimes one of the clergy will read a paper on some current problem and there will be a discussion. Sometimes there will be a general binding and grousing session about 'them' at the centre, how 'they' waste our time by sending us forms to fill in and generally prevent us getting on with our proper work. The clergy chapter, which I joined when I was appointed to my first parish, spent every session for two years grumbling about the 'quota', which is the money each parish is asked to send to the diocese. I mention this not to join in the popular game of pulling the clergy to pieces. As will emerge later, I have a profound admiration for and belief in my fellow clergy. But I mention it first of all to show that we are much like other people and secondly to pinpoint the number one problem of the Church of England which this chapter is all about.

When the Bishop appointed me Diocesan Missioner it seemed obvious that my first job was to get to know the clergy. It would be silly to dash all over the diocese preaching high-powered gospel sermons. This is what people expect, rather apprehensively, that a diocesan missioner is going to do. But I was faced with the uncomfortable fact that I didn't really know what the gospel was – I didn't really know what 'good news' God was trying to get through at that particular moment to the Coventry Diocese. And I knew that in that diocese were 200 dedicated clergy, each rooted in the reality of a parish, who were far more likely to know than I was.

So I determined to go round the chapters and meet the clergy, to talk as little as possible and to *listen* carefully, and to try to hear the answer to this question, 'What is the Spirit saying to the churches?'

One of my first visits was to the Monks Kirby Chapter. It is a group of about ten clergy whose parishes stretch from the new housing estates on the edge of Coventry to the little village of Monks Kirby with its glorious mediaeval church. Our meeting was fixed for 10.30 am on 17th February 1959 and it is here my story starts.

After prayers and introductions I asked my colleagues to tell me what they thought were the special problems and opportunities facing us. During the conversation one of them said:

'We are faced with the consecration of our Cathedral in just over three years. I believe this is going to be a great spiritual opportunity.'

There was a pause.

'An opportunity for what?' someone asked. 'How can it be more than a great festival and a blowing of trumpets?'

The discussion started and we very soon came to see that what God wanted was not just a consecrated Cathedral, but a *consecrated people* living round it. And there followed quickly the second uncomfortable discovery, that if there was to be a consecrated people, it would have to begin with ourselves.

So we decided to go away together for a 'quiet day', in order to ask God a question and listen for the answer. The question was:

'What does it mean to be a consecrated people? And what, in particular, O Lord God who created the universe, do you want the Monks Kirby Chapter to do now?'

We gathered in a country parish on a summer morning and the programme was Holy Communion, breakfast, Bible study and silence, lunch, discussion. All these were important elements in what happened. To come home together in Holy Communion to the House of God, to eat meals in company, to listen to God's word springing fresh out of the Bible, and to be silent, these are things which satisfy at a deep level.

When we came to the discussion time after lunch, we sat under a crab apple tree in the garden and we asked each other: 'Well, what has God said to us? What answer has he given to our question?'

Nothing emerged very clearly till one said, 'You know, it's very good to get together like this.'

Everyone agreed, and an old priest bordering on his eightieth birthday said, 'I think we ought to do it every week.'

The others laughed, for this was clearly impossible. Parish priests are far too busy. They carry a tremendous burden of work. Many people still believe that a minister only works on Sunday, but the truth is that many work sixteen hours a day, seven days a week. It is not just a question of praying, leading worship in church and preaching sermons, though this is exacting enough if you are to have something fresh and compelling to say each week. There is the whole outreach of the love of Jesus Christ, in visiting the sick and caring for people in all their problems; to say nothing of the baptisms, weddings and funerals, each one of which matters infinitely, the training of new Christians, and the organisation of all the clubs which express the family life of the Church, and are its method of serving the community.

So these people laughed. They knew they simply hadn't time to meet weekly, to pray together, to read the Bible together, to be silent, and to discuss.

But now the truth began to dawn upon us. We had come away to a quiet place, to ask God what he wanted us to do. He had told us. His answer was simple, obvious, yet revolutionary and costly: 'Meet weekly'.

So there could be no more talk of impossibility. This is what the Monks Kirby Chapter must do. They must do what they were told, for there is nothing more dangerous than to hear the word of God and not to do it. So they decided to meet the following Monday from 9 am to 10 am and every Monday morning for three months. After three months they would review the position.

But when three months were over, the position was so changed as to be hardly recognisable. The chapter consisted no longer of a number of isolated parish priests, each battling on heroically alone. It had become a team who knew one another, cared about one another, belonged to one another, and most important of all, had begun to admit to one another their own weaknesses.

We must stop for a moment and face some unpleasant facts, and begin to understand what a revolution is described in that last paragraph. The importance of it will become clear as the book goes on, and in Part Two I shall comment upon it and try to indicate some of the radical changes in Church life towards which I believe it points us. But for the moment, let me just record a typical conversation at the beginning of a chapter meeting, at a time when I was a young priest just launched onto a new housing estate.

'Good morning, Verney. How's the parish going?'

'Very well, thank you. And yours?'

'Oh, yes! All going well.'

And so we would smile affably and each sit down feeling rather jealous of the other. I, because I knew I was failing. I knew I was faced with a gigantic task, before which I was bewildered and inadequate, and I supposed that this older man really *was* doing well in his parish. He knew the ropes, he had an easy approach to youth, and he understood how to speak to people in moments of bereavement. And he, poor man, knowing only too well that he was growing old, and the fire had gone from his belly, saw in me an arrogant young chap who was being successful. So we never met one another. We never encouraged one another. We never helped one another in the work of God, because we dared not admit to one another our failures and stand together at that point of need where the Christian life and true Christian work begins.

But in the Monks Kirby Chapter, something different had begun to happen. The clergy were a mixed bunch, one of whom was very 'high', and talked about the Mass and heard confessions. When he wrote to me his letter began 'Dear Father'. Another was very 'low' and ran in his parish many excellent Bible study groups. His letters began 'Dear Brother'. A third was a keen supporter of Moral Re-armament.

As the weekly meetings continued, Monday after Monday, these clergy grew less and less suspicious of each other. As they studied the Bible together, and each spoke of the truth as they saw it, they began first to know that the other was genuine, and then to discover that each had something to teach them which they hadn't quite grasped before. As they knelt together in prayer, perhaps above all as they were silent, they began to know that they belonged to one another and cared about each other's work, and that the mighty task to which they were committed, and which was overwhelming them individually, was something they could tackle together in a strength greater than their own.

About a year later, they had reached a point of brotherly love where each was allowing a sermon to be tape-recorded and then played back to the others for their criticism!

And a young curate, who had just been appointed to one of those parishes, made this comment:

'My fellow students from theological college who have gone to other parts of the country say how they envy me when I write and tell them what is going on here. They are involved in all the normal tensions and lack of charity between parishes, but here we seem to be a sort of fellowship of the Holy Spirit.'

Chapter 2

Balliol

During the autumn of 1959 the Monks Kirby Chapter wrote to the Bishop to tell him what was happening. He called a meeting of his staff and of the other clergy with special responsibility in the diocese. He asked them to come away with him for three days, to live and eat and pray and talk together, and to discuss the whole question of preparations for 1962 and the consecration of the Cathedral.

To that meeting we made a full report of the Monks Kirby discoveries and urged the Bishop to write round to the other chapters and to lay upon them that they too should begin to organise themselves into a similar pattern.

'We have only three years and there is no time to be lost.'

When we had finished, there was a long silence and that silence proved to be one of the hinges in this whole story. After a while the Bishop said,

'No, I won't lay anything on. If this thing is really of the Holy Spirit, it will bubble up from underneath.'

And the Archdeacon of Warwick, who was sitting next to him, added,

'From my slight acquaintance with the Holy Spirit, I believe that he will not be stereotyped and he will not be hurried.'

Perhaps this is the moment to introduce Bishop Cuthbert of Coventry to those readers who do not know him personally and have not seen him on television. The whole creative movement in his diocese during these last years has been made possible by his leadership. He is a man of prayer and he has the gift of friendship, which enables everybody else to relax and become themselves, and sets them free to use whatever talents they have. All that this book describes is only the outworking of his vision, by which he saw, from the moment he was appointed Bishop, that his diocese must before all else be a family. Few people in England can speak more powerfully about the Christian faith to ordinary men and women, but his real leadership lies in this deeper quality, that round him as a centre, people find themselves drawn into friendship with each other.

So on that morning he refused to impose anything on his clergy by authority, but he suggested that the Chapter Clerk of Monks Kirby (the 'high' Father whom by now I had come to know as Jack) should write to all the other chapters, and ask for a chance to meet them and tell them our story.

There are thirteen rural deaneries in the Coventry Diocese, and about eleven of them invited us along. Of these, about nine decided that they, too, must begin as the Monks Kirby Chapter had begun and must go away together for a quiet day of prayer and discussion to find out how they could become more clearly consecrated. (What of those who didn't ask us, and who didn't respond in any visible way? In most cases I believe that the Holy Spirit was already proving that he 'would not be stereotyped'. But in one case it was due to a parish priest who took the 'I'm all right, Jack' line, and argued convincingly to his colleagues that they were consecrated already, by their ordination vows, and needed nothing more.)

The days of prayer took place during that winter. A little group of clergy would arrive at a village church and begin with a

Fire in Coventry / The Story

celebration of the Holy Communion. Silence was usually kept till after lunch and while we ate together someone would read to us. During the morning there were usually two short addresses on a Bible text. I remember one such day spent during an icy spell, when the heating in the village church seemed hardly to lift the temperature above freezing point. Our breath made clouds in the cold air, and during the times of prayer the Rural Dean marched up and down the aisle, stamping his feet and beating his breast, not so much in an agony of contrition as in a failure of circulation. I mention these things to emphasise that this was no time of emotion, but rather of honest people trying to discover what God wanted them to do.

The conclusion they came to was in every case that they were being commanded to *meet*, though in every case they decided on a different pattern of meeting. The Coventry Chapter, which consisted of about forty clergy, decided to split up into three groups. Other chapters decided to meet together as a body, some weekly, others at longer intervals. The time of meeting was the greatest obstacle of all, for it is indeed true that the parish clergy are too busy. There was one occasion when every hour of the week seemed to be impossible for somebody, and they decided finally on once a week at 7 am. For one, this meant leaving home at 6.30 am on a winter morning, but it seemed to them clear that they had been given an order and that a sacrifice must be made to carry it out.

By the time the spring of 1960 was stirring in the lanes and woods of Warwickshire, it was obvious that some new thing was also stirring amongst the clergy. The sap was rising with the promise of new life, to flower in ways we could not yet see, and to bear fruit whose texture and shape and flavour we could not yet know.

So the Bishop decided that the following autumn he must gather a conference of all his clergy, to try and discover what God had been saying to us and what we should do together to prepare the whole diocese for the consecration of 1962.

We met in September, at Balliol College, Oxford, about 180 of us. The Bishop had asked me to speak on the first evening and to present to the conference a plan of action for the next eighteen months. Then we were to turn our attention to one of the most important questions confronting the church today and Dr Kathleen Bliss was to be our chief speaker on *The Laity*.

There is something rather daunting about clerical collars, and I must confess that I was terrified at the idea of addressing 180 of them. Only by now I had begun to know the hearts that beat below the collars and the heads that emerged up out of them. They had in fact become to me, and I to them, real people. And so it was possible to say that evening, in that circle of friends, what may now appear to be criticism when committed to the cold printed page of a book.

I told the story, more or less as I have told it again in these last two chapters, of how the clergy had been led to meet. Then I went on to report the results of our *listening* to what the Spirit had been saying to the churches:

> Several deaneries have been meeting now for varying lengths of time. Some have allowed the meetings to drop off. But where we have gone on, I think that one truth has gradually emerged, so crashingly platitudinous that we kick ourselves and wonder how on earth we had the face to pose as Christian leaders before we saw it.
>
> A NEW COMMANDMENT I GIVE UNTO YOU, the new commandment at the heart of my kingdom, the new commandment without which there can be no kingdom, THAT YE LOVE ONE ANOTHER AS I HAVE LOVED YOU, that is with a deep self-giving compassion.

We have begun to discover that we must take definite steps and give up time to make this possible, and that where we do, where we fuse together, a new power is generated. We have begun to see that we can't afford to go on quarrelling or failing in positive compassion amongst ourselves. Until these differences are frankly faced and put away, and we have come to know and trust one another, all our church work is sounding brass and clanging cymbals.

This I would like to submit to your judgement, as being what God has said to us during this last year and the clue to what we must do in the next two … If this is right, and we all agree, then let us go ahead with the confidence of people to whom God has spoken.

Now for the future. The plan! Following the clue of the past year, this plan is not presented to or imposed upon the clergy. It has emerged from the clergy. Already at least 100 clergy have been consulted about it. The ideas in it have been contributed by all sorts of people. Now it is brought before this conference for your final hammering into shape, and so that you can then lay it before God for three days in prayer.

The Plan

We then examined the plan, which was in everybody's hands on a duplicated sheet of paper. It embodied the idea that when a stone falls into the centre of a pond, the ripples expand over the surface in ever widening circles. So a stone had fallen into the midst of our diocese, and the *first ripple* had been the clergy. Now we must plan for the gathering in of the laity in three ever widening circles.

The *second ripple*, we suggested, should be groups of clergy and laity meeting together from October 1960 to Easter 1961. Three parishes should combine, and each parish priest bring with them three lay people. This would make an ideal discussion group, twelve strong, with three clergy and nine laity. Here are the notes, just as they appeared on the conference paper:

> Get laity to tell us how they see the church and what needs doing. Listen before we talk. How can clergy and laity help one another? Get off our pedestals. Admit we are only on the threshold of understanding. Painful meeting necessary. Radical and revolutionary questions asked. Listen to criticism, accept and absorb it. Let LAY perspective be revealed. Let groups be open to the Spirit to make adventures (if led) in prayer and obedience.

The result of this ripple, we hoped, would be the forming of a nucleus of four convinced people to go back together into the parish where the vision had got to be worked out.

The *third ripple* should be the congregation of each parish from Easter 1961 to Palm Sunday 1962. We envisaged that in each parish its own individual plan must emerge, different according to its needs, but the year would be used by us all to prepare for definite, concrete acts of obedience and prayer in which the whole diocese would be involved at the time of the consecration of the Cathedral.

So in general, we would have parish schools to learn about our *baptismal vows* and about *prayer*. These schools would not be run as lectures, but as group discussions, so that we might all continue to listen to one another. And if, during this year, our schools spilt over into evangelism, as we hoped they might, then let it be the opposite of what is generally thought of as evangelism. Let our laity learn to listen and let the world tell the Church, for true evangelism begins with prayer, humility, listening and service.

The *fourth ripple* should be the gathering up of the whole diocese for certain dramatic acts:

- Forty days and forty nights of prayer, as the Cathedral Cross of Nails is carried round the parishes, Palm Sunday to 25th May 1962.
- The re-affirming of our baptismal and ordination vows.
- The consecration of the Cathedral, 26th May 1962.

The *fifth ripple*. We saw that the whole of this mighty programme would only bring us to a starting point. But a starting point towards what? Nobody could foresee. I find in my old battered copy of that conference paper these words scribbled:

'God alone knows.'

Dr Kathleen Bliss

But God, of course, did know. And now there happened one of those astonishing coincidences in which we can recognise him at work.

On the very next day of our conference, a laywoman of the Church of England stood up and declared to us, with prophetic insight, all those truths after which we had been groping.

She pointed first to the obvious fact that 99.5 per cent of the Church consists of laity, not clergy. They are the *people of God*, scattered through the world, six days out of seven, being husbands and wives, fathers and mothers, neighbours, workers, citizens. Their work is the greater part of their life.

But the Church does not help them to grasp the exciting vision of *who they are*. The laity find it difficult to speak to the clergy about their fundamental doubts and to admit how little they know. They think that the clergy accept everything without question and would be shocked to discover that this was not so. What we need are real meeting points between laity and clergy. The sermon cannot be the central point of teaching, for it can only support teaching and discussion and Bible study that is going on elsewhere. What we need are occasions when we can *listen* to each other.

She told us of a fascinating book *Is Anybody Listening?* by William Whyte, which describes how information passes down, or fails to pass down, in industry. What are the conditions of a manager being heard by his workers? One clear answer emerges. *The ability to be heard depends on the capacity to listen.* If a manager is listening at all levels of his firm, then he will be heard right down to the bottom.

This is a truth we must discover in the Church. We must devise a system by which we can listen. We must make the sort of group in the parish where not only the minister listens to the laity, but the laity listen to each other. Listen, and understand, with sympathetic imagination. We all long to believe that our job has a meaning, and we love to talk about it to somebody else who thinks it matters. As we talk together we come to understand how we are all missionaries in our places of work, 'the people of God scattered through the world'. When this exciting truth breaks upon the laity, they come to need the clergy as never before. They want to be taught to pray, in a way that fits the conditions of daily life. They want to re-learn, at a deeper level, the faith of their childhood and their youth, so that it becomes an 'all-out personal involvement, for keeps, with Christ and his Church'.

So Dr Kathleen Bliss sowed in our minds seed thoughts. We forgot them. I have only remembered that she said these things by turning up an old notebook of the conference. But seeds, buried in the earth, break surface at the proper time, and what she said that day flowered and bore fruit in the following year, as I shall describe in the next chapter. What she prophesied exactly happened.

The End of the Conference

On the last evening we returned to the plan. This had been discussed in small groups and was now debated publicly. There were hesitations on the part of a few, but the plan was generally accepted by the whole body of clergy, with one exception. This man spoke violently against it. He said he didn't hold with all this talk of getting off pedestals. A priest was a priest and he should teach and the laity should accept his teaching.

Later that evening he came to understand that his objections had sprung from his own sense of insecurity and by the time the clocks struck midnight the clergy of the Coventry Diocese, though many of them fast asleep, 'were *all with one accord in one place*' (Acts 2:1).

Chapter 3

The Clergy–Laity Groups

Twelve chairs round a fire on a winter evening. Filling three of them, clergy. Sitting on the edge of the other nine, laymen and women. The second ripple on the pond had begun.

But by the end of that first evening we were all sitting back at our ease. For on opening our little booklets of study notes, we found that we were advised to spend our first evening getting to know one another.

The author of these brilliant study notes was Canon Edward Patey of Coventry Cathedral and the success of our clergy–laity groups was largely due to his guidance. Even more important than what he asked us to study, was *how* he asked us to study.

'These notes,' he wrote, 'are intended as signposts, not tram-lines! They suggest the direction in which groups might care to explore; they are not meant to restrict the direction of the Spirit.'

He then advised us how each group must discover its own pace for working and not be bound to any time schedule, how we should abandon the notes altogether if we began to develop our own line of thought, and finally, how we should 'aim at a free and easy conversation, with all taking part. Clergy and laity are all learners and explorers. The one leader of the group is the Holy Spirit.'

But the most helpful advice of all was that we should spend the first evening getting to know one another. We had arrived from three different parishes and this meant we were strangers to each other. In some cases, we disapproved of the other parish's churchmanship. In the country we started with that deep prejudice that every village has about its neighbour. But this was not all. Some members of the group were executive types and some were working class. Some were old, and some were members of the youth club. Most difficult of all, some were clergy! We had all arrived rather tense and shy and expecting that we should have to talk about our Christian faith, which to most English people is embarrassing.

But on that first evening, no one mentioned God and no one spoke of Jesus Christ. We went round the circle and each one spoke about themselves. They gave their Christian name and surname, and told us if they were married and had children. We learnt about their past history, their jobs, their hobbies and interests. By the end, we had become twelve real people to each other and we were all marvelling at the range of personality and experience gathered round that fireside. A retired air force officer, a man with a beard who ran a laundry, a girl from a factory, a young farmer, an accountant, a farmer's wife, an engineer, a schoolmistress, the mother of a family – these were our nine laity, and with them were not just three anonymous clergy, but three living people, also with Christian names and families, one of whom had served in India, another in the West Indies, and the third had been disguised as a Cretan peasant in the resistance movement.

We had begun to know one another. But something even more significant had happened. After listening in that friendly circle to eleven people talking about themselves, we had experienced a deep sense of the presence of God. If his name had been mentioned, I do not believe we should have experienced his presence. We had first to relax and know one another before we could together know him.

From this beginning, the group launched out on the second evening to discuss 'What is the church in my parish really for?' This got everyone talking and when we had all given our rather idealistic views of what the church ought to be like, we were faced with the next question, 'But is it in fact like that?'

Then came the criticisms. 'Sermons boring and too long ... psalms impossible to sing ... ministers out of touch ... people think only of money.' And after the criticisms, a growing humility, an understanding of the other's difficulty, and the discovery that what is really wrong with the Church is me.

> What sort of a Church would my church be
> If everyone in the Church was just like me?

And after the humility, the real thing which made these groups so exciting: the deep, rich, growing sense of Christian fellowship.

As the year went on, a few of us went round visiting the groups to try and gather some general impression of what was happening. What was the Spirit saying to the churches? One thing came back to us from every single group without exception, which was the astonishing and extraordinary experience of fellowship. It was unlike anything we had known before. Barriers had gone between parishes, between old and young, rich and poor, 'high' and 'low', and above all between clergy and laity. We were really meeting each other and coming to know ourselves as a team, who must do the work of God together.

The laity had come to see, with a shock, that they were the *front line soldiers of the Church*. They, not the clergy, were the representatives of Christ who were actually present in the factories, shops, offices, schools and homes of the country. If Christ's compassion was to get into those situations, then they, the laity, must be the channels through which it would come. If Christ's truth was to be spoken, then they must speak it.

Suddenly they felt rather weak at the knees. How could they, selfish, proud, lustful, ill-tempered creatures, be the channels of Christ's compassion? How could they speak his truth, which they did not understand? And so it began to pour out – the utter, bewildered ignorance of the laity about the Christian faith, those elementary questions they had always been ashamed to ask, those doubts they had fought against and never dared to express. And in face of their honest questions, an honest answer from the clergy:

> We too understand very little about the Christian faith. We are like children paddling on the edge of an ocean. We, too, doubt. But perhaps through our doubting and our wrestling, and because God really does open the door when men and women beat desperately and continuously upon it, we have got a little further in understanding, and this we can share with you.

So there began to emerge a new clergy–laity pattern. The laity, seeing themselves as front line soldiers of the Church, needed the clergy as never before. They needed teaching so that they could speak Christ's truth. They needed the sacraments, so that they could know Christ's forgiveness and love, and pass it on to others. The clergy began to see their job in new terms, first and foremost as people of prayer supporting these active-service soldiers and then as trainers and teachers of an eager laity, standing beside them in their doubts, understanding sympathetically the problems of their working lives, exploring and learning with them the meaning of love and of prayer.

But in describing these groups, I must not give the impression that they were a 'success'. They went much, much deeper than that. Alongside the exhilarating experience of fellowship, there went in every case a feeling of frustration. One group summed it up like this: 'We feel like the first Christians after Easter and before Pentecost.'

What did they mean by that?

First, they had passed through a shaking of the foundations. One priest I know was physically in tears after a group meeting because he had come to see how shallow had been his whole ministry up to that moment. One laywoman (there may well have been others) gave up the meetings, because she dared not face the new truth which was springing up at her.

Secondly, they had experienced the joy of Christ in the midst and the sense of forgiveness one towards another. But they felt something was missing. It was all very well sitting cosily round the fire, but they didn't want to become a pious clique. There was a great work to be done, but what exactly was that work? And how should they discover the power to carry it through?

So the groups, one by one, were driven to prayer. Not the sort of prayer which is often described like this in the parish magazine, 'After the vicar had thanked the ladies who had so kindly provided the tea, he closed with prayer', but prayer that arose out of the group because they had a hearty desire to pray. Some groups learnt to pray *extempore*, each member expressing in simple words whatever was in their mind. Some learnt to wait upon God in silence. Some learnt how to bring their prayers to the focal point of the Holy Communion.

This was the second word which God seemed to be saying to us. If the first had been 'love one another', the second was 'pray'. Every group reached the first point, but many dried up because they failed to reach the second. What the Spirit seemed to be saying to the churches was this, 'I want companies of Christians who will love one another as Jesus loved them, and who will recognise their need for God, and put themselves together at his disposal.'

Love, humility, prayer. Where these came together the groups began exploding. The first to explode was in a remote country district where two of the vicars concerned were old and the third had a groggy heart. This was the last place in the world where you might have expected religious revival. Surely it would come where the clergy could give dynamic leadership? But no, it came out of this situation of love, humility and prayer. The lay people in this group were so excited by what was happening that they summoned a public meeting. They hired a hall and a band. The Rural Dean, hearing about it, rang up in some anxiety and suggested that the whole thing was getting out of hand! Out of whose hand? For when the meeting took place, these laymen and women spoke simply about their rediscovery of the Christian faith and those who had come to listen were moved by their words.

A few weeks later another group followed suit. They called a public meeting, spoke from the platform and answered questions. A young farmer, with no sort of theological training, was answering difficult questions graciously and with an astonishing insight. After the meeting somebody who had been there said to me, 'I know now how fishermen from Galilee were able to confound the Jewish Sanhedrin.' (The Sanhedrin was the council of religious leaders by whom Peter and John were examined shortly after the day of Pentecost. Peter spoke to them 'filled with the Holy Spirit'. And we read that 'as they observed the boldness of Peter and John and noted that they were untrained laymen, they began to wonder' (Acts 4:13).)

Chapter 4

In the Parishes

'From my slight acquaintance with the Holy Spirit, I believe he will not be stereotyped and he will not be hurried.' So the Archdeacon of Warwick had warned us.

In describing the second ripple on the pond, the clergy–laity group, I have made it sound as if there was a neat pattern. This was not so. Each group was different and it was only when we visited the groups, listened to their own reports on themselves, and collated them, that we discovered the very general pattern which I have outlined in the last chapter.

But now, as we come to the third ripple on the pond – the group in the parishes – the outstanding impression is of a glorious riot and confusion, like spring bursting in a thousand different patterns out of bulbs and roots and twigs. Nothing that happened in one parish was quite like anything in another. All you could say was that it was still the same springtime.

And if the Holy Spirit would not be stereotyped, neither would he be hurried. According to 'the plan', this last winter before the consecration of the Cathedral was Stage Three. But about this time many parishes embarked on Stage Two, and one rural deanery awoke to Stage One, claiming that up to this moment nobody had told them anything about it.

Where parish groups did meet, you could not be sure what they might be studying. Canon Patey had produced another study outline about our baptismal vows, which we should be invited to affirm at special services at the time of the Cathedral's consecration. But some parishes wanted to do last year's study all over again, with a wider circle. Others branched out on lines of their own. Others continued to do nothing. It was as though, because of this thing which was coming to birth in our midst, each individual parish was reacting according to its own nature. Each was becoming more truly itself.

Here, then, are one or two glimpses into this rich and burgeoning confusion:

First, a new housing-estate parish in Coventry, where the vicar has the care of about 7,000 people. After the summer holidays of 1961 he, and the three who had been with him in the clergy–laity group, met with his Parochial Church Council. He rang up a friend after the meeting and said, 'I just had to talk to someone. This has been the most wonderful meeting since I was ordained.' They had hatched a plan by which ten lay people would become leaders of groups in their own houses. They would invite their friends along and lead the discussions and only ask the vicar to come and join them when they really needed him. These groups met monthly throughout the whole of that winter. The leaders also met monthly with the vicar to prepare for their next session and report to him how things were going.

Someone who took part describes what happened: 'We started with a wonderful atmosphere. Then people began to realise that it would demand a lot of them. Some gave up. 'This is all too serious for me,' they said. Others came to know the real challenge of the Christian faith: 'You can go on for too long being an ordinary member of a parish without being challenged personally. And what we found ourselves challenged to do was not necessarily in the parish, but in our lives. Not to be *busy*, but to convert our lives, to turn to more kindly thoughts and things like that.'

Here is another glimpse: this time a country parish with only a few hundred inhabitants. During the winter of 1961–62 up to thirty people used to pack into the vicar's dining room once a week. The problem here was, not to get people to a meeting, but that too many had come really to *meet*. Inevitably a few powerful talkers began to dominate the discussion and the shy people never opened their mouths. And so the vicar firmly split them into three groups. After introducing the subject for discussion, he sent ten to his study and ten to his drawing room, leaving ten in the dining room. He himself sat on the stairs for half an hour in the middle of his own house, while all round him furious theological discussion broke loose. At the end of the allotted time, he rang a bell but nobody moved. He would go to each room and peal the bell in their ears. 'Go away, for goodness sake,' they said, 'we haven't nearly finished'.

A third glimpse: this time it is the Church of England's Men's Society (CEMS) meeting in a little county town. They are a dozen men who want to serve Christ and his Church. Usually they invite a speaker to their society meetings and every secretary knows what a headache it is to find speakers to fill up all the gaps in next year's programme. And be it whispered: though the speakers are usually interesting and 'a very nice evening is had by all', they don't often seem to get us anywhere. They are not answering on our own wavelength the real questions that arise out of our own daily lives. How can they, for they have never met us before? So in that winter of 1961, this branch of the CEMS passed a resolution that they would have no outside speakers for a year. Instead, they and their vicar would talk to each other and listen to each other. (Six months later that group made themselves responsible for an all-night vigil of prayer, such as you will read about in chapter 6, and in the small hours of the morning told their vicar quite firmly to go to bed, and leave them to it.)

Many other stories could be told of groups that petered out and came to nothing, and we learnt as much from the 'failures' as from the 'successes'. What cried aloud was this, that group discussion is by no means easy. The leader is all important and many groups failed because we clergy exercised either too much leadership or too little. Some of us dominated, so that the laity never really discussed. Others were so humble that they would assert no authority at all and then the powerful personalities in the group spoilt everything by talking too much and refusing to listen.

What was being demanded of us was a new technique of leadership that blends speaking with listening, that knows how to get others both to speak and to listen, and so set free the truth of God that can spring out of the heart of a company of friends. In fact, we were learning what Canon Patey had meant when he wrote 'the one leader of the group is the Holy Spirit'. And we were beginning to understand what Jesus meant when he said, 'When he comes who is the Holy Spirit of truth, he will guide you into all the truth; for he will not speak on his own authority, but will tell only what he hears' (John 16:13).

Chapter 5

The Bishop's Mission

We have now arrived in our story at 1962, the year of the consecration of Coventry Cathedral, and at the fourth ripple on the
pond when the whole diocese began to be gathered up in certain
dramatic events.

When we had planned these events two years before, there
was no talk of a Bishop's mission. The first hint came to me in a
letter from the Bishop dated 25th March 1961. 'Could you possibly
stay on after the meeting on Monday, as I very much want to see
you about a most important matter relating to next Lent.' He took
me out in the garden and told me of an idea that had come to him
in his time of prayer that a few weeks before the consecration he
should lead a mission to the diocese.

One thing was immediately clear to him, that this should not
be a 'diocesan mission', in the sense that every parish should
hold its own mission services. Rather, he himself, in one central
church, would preach the gospel for ten evenings in succession. As
the Father of the family, he would gather his own people round
him. As he put it a month later at the diocesan conference, 'We
are thinking in terms of the consecration of a people. It is my hope
and belief that these mission services will lead many to put their

whole trust unreservedly in the Lord Jesus Christ and to accept him as their Lord and saviour.'

The next point was not so clear. To whom was his preaching to be addressed? Some twenty of us, clergy and lay, who had been asked to form a mission team, were equally divided on this issue. Half of us thought he should speak to those who do not normally come to church. The other half thought equally firmly that he should speak to the regular and faithful churchgoers, so that they might become infectiously Christian. The second of these alternatives was what overwhelmingly happened.

During the summer and autumn we planned the details. It was agreed that the main services should be held at All Saints Church, Leamington Spa, which holds 2,000 people. But nobody could guess how many people would turn up. Some said we should never fill such a big church for ten nights. Others foresaw that there would be vast crowds and overflow meetings. In the event we had just about 20,000 people to seat at the ten mission services and though some nights were 'standing room only', we never had to turn anyone away.

Posters were designed to be displayed all over the diocese. A prayer card was sent out to some thousands of people, including many of the religious communities (the monks, friars and nuns of the Church of England who, unseen, support so much of our work in prayer).

But the most important preparation was the training of nearly 200 counsellors. The Bishop was intending to end each address with an appeal that any who wished might come forward and dedicate their lives afresh to God. He wanted to have men and women ready, at this moment, to meet those who had made such an act of dedication, to offer them friendship and encouragement, and to help them if necessary to contact their parish priest and find their way into the church. About 200 accepted his invitation to be trained for this work. They were a remarkable crowd, men and women, young and old, and during the weeks leading up to the mission they were most brilliantly trained by Captain Tom Reeman of the Church Army for this sensitive work. And here we began to discover that a mission achieves most through its by-products. For these 200 meeting together in discussion and Bible study and prayer, brought to a deep humility and a new dependence on God, learning to love and to listen — these 200 themselves passed through an experience of conversion and dedication, and became a powerful instrument in the hand of God and at the heart of the diocese.

Now 1962 had arrived. The mission was planned for 4th to 14th April. During January and February the Bishop toured the diocese, meeting all the leaders both clergy and lay, and kindling enthusiasm as he went. A meeting was held in every one of the thirteen rural deaneries. Each parish of the deanery was represented by its clergy and parochial council and other leading personalities, and there might be between 100 and 200 people present. The Bishop asked me to outline, in the first half of the meeting, what had been happening in the diocese and what was about to happen, so that everyone could be fully informed and could make suggestions. It would be difficult to exaggerate the importance of this. It broke down the barrier between 'them' at the centre and 'us' in the parishes. Everybody knew what was going on and many valuable suggestions were made which were put into effect during the next three months and helped the events to run smoothly.

Then the Bishop himself spoke. 'Why,' he asked, 'a mission at this particular time?' He explained his own deep conviction that the people of the world were hungry for God. But on the whole they were not turning to the Church. Why was this? Because they did not see in the churches a body of people filled with love. He went on to emphasise the great opportunity of the coming year, when Coventry Diocese would be the centre of world interest. People would be coming from all over the world, but what would they find? A humdrum, ordinary church? Or a church alert, alive, attuned to God's purpose? Would they find, above all, a diocese of converted people? He talked to us about conversion; about the moment when we come to know that God loves us, and we commit our lives to him; about the fruits of the Spirit which are to be seen in converted people, an inner peace, a joy, a love that goes out to the last and the lost and the least. Finally, he gave details of the mission and encouraged his listeners to prepare for it and come to it.

When the Bishop had finished speaking, we had on each occasion a remarkable period of prayer. 'I am going to ask you,' he said, 'to do what you have probably never done before in your life. To pray out loud, in your own words. We shall wait upon God in silence, and each of us is free to offer up prayers as we wish.'

Silence fell, embarrassed, tense – for Anglicans are not used to this sort of thing. Then one would pray and the floodgates would be open and from all over the room would come prayer from the heart, whether expressed in a few halting words, or in the well-loved cadences of a Prayer Book collect. Once, nobody was willing to begin. The Bishop prayed. I prayed. Then there was a long agonising silence. Suddenly the Bishop roared out, 'O God, forgive us our cowardice!' This appeared to unlock the situation, and a woman in the front row prayed and was followed by others. After the meeting she came up to the Bishop quite exhilarated, and was one of the many who told him that this experience had brought them to a new sense of the reality of prayer.

Again we were witnessing a by-product of the mission. Each of these thirteen preparatory meetings was like a little mission in itself, and as the leaders of the diocese met their Bishop, the whole family was being drawn together, powerfully and invisibly, into the fellowship of love.

But was this a by-product? As 4th to 14th April came and went, we discovered that it was in fact the heart and meaning of the whole operation.

From all over Warwickshire cars and coaches converged on All Saints, Leamington. The people who came crowding into the church were not coming out of curiosity, as they might have done if a famous stranger had been speaking; they were coming to hear their own well-known and well-beloved Bishop. And they were not, on the whole, people from outside the Church. There were a few from the fringe, but most of those women and men, boys and girls, filling the pews and overflowing into the chancel and even into the sanctuary, were the regular faithful churchgoers of the parishes of the diocese.

Before the service began, all those who were leading the worship and acting as counsellors gathered for fifteen minutes of prayer in the vestry, led by the Archdeacon of Warwick. We put ourselves at the disposal of God to be used by him, opened our minds to the theme of that evening's preaching and prayed for the blessing of the Holy Spirit upon us all who were to listen. These last moments together seemed to focus and let loose the power of all the prayer that had been offered up in the county in the preceding months.

The service was as follows: two or three opening hymns, while the latecomers found their places, and then a short talk by myself on the theme of *Perseverance in prayer*. I tried to expound the teaching of Jesus about prayer and in particular his promise that if we would only slog away at it, we should in the end discover that the Holy Spirit was praying from inside us. This part of the service ended with us all saying together the prayer:

O Holy Ghost, giver of light and life;
>> Impart to us thoughts higher than our own thoughts,
>> And prayers better than our own prayers,
>> And powers beyond our own powers;
> That we may spend and be spent in the ways of love and
> Goodness, after the perfect image of our Lord and
> Saviour Jesus Christ.[1]

Then after another hymn the Bishop mounted the pulpit, dressed simply in a cassock, and spoke to us for thirty or forty minutes about faith. He declared to us the old, deep truths about the love of God and how we respond to it and how we can find strength to live it out in our daily lives. As each address came to an end he led us in prayer and then invited anyone who so wished to remain behind and to make a simple act of dedicating his or her life to God. If there were any who felt called to ordination or to devote the whole of their lives to some positive kind of service, they were asked to wait behind in the side chapel.

During the ten evenings, 220 accepted the invitation to make an act of dedication. This might seem at first sight rather meagre and disappointing. We had secretly hoped that many more would be pierced to the heart and come forward to accept Jesus Christ as their Lord. But when we saw *who* was coming forward, then we understood that God was answering our prayers in a way very different from what we had expected and far more wonderfully.

For example, from my own parish five people went forward. They were two churchwardens, an ex-churchwarden and two others who were already deeply dedicated. These were the kind of people whom God seemed to be calling through the Bishop's words. After they had knelt and prayed and offered their lives afresh to God, they each met a counsellor with whom they talked and exchanged addresses and who gave them a card to sign and take away which said:

TONIGHT GOD HAS SHOWN ME:
>   That my faith in Jesus has not been sufficiently alive.
>   That he offers me forgiveness and new life.
THIS I GRATEFULLY ACCEPT.

I KNOW THAT IN THIS SPIRIT
OF GRATITUDE I MUST:
- Pray and read my Bible every day.
- Share fully in the worship life and fellowship of the Church.
- Be loyal to Jesus by word and deed, at home, at work, and in the world.

Meanwhile, in the side chapel, something even more remarkable was happening. Amongst those who came to enquire about full-time service were three young women offering themselves for work overseas, two middle-aged women who would equip themselves for teaching, and a steady stream of men of all ages, from their teens to late middle-age, to ask about ordination. Of these, ten have so far definitely offered themselves as a result of the call of God which they heard at that time.

Two things had become clear by the end of the mission. The more deeply people were involved, the more clearly was God calling them to go deeper still and to offer him the obedience of their whole lives. This was the first unmistakable answer to our prayers.

And a second was this. During those ten days, *the diocese became a person, a body alive with a spirit.* As we gathered in our thousands at one central point round our Bishop – as he spoke to us God's word and convinced us of God's love – as he led us in prayer and the offering of our lives, an extraordinary happiness broke through. We became a loving family with a purpose. In a few weeks our new Cathedral was to be consecrated, but something revolutionary had already happened. 'Surely you know that you are God's temple, where the Spirit of God dwells' (1 Corinthians 3:16).

---

1   From *My God My Glory*, by E. Milner-White.

Chapter 6

The Cross of Nails

When Coventry Cathedral was blitzed in November 1940 and destroyed by fire, a large number of mediaeval nails were found amongst the rubble and sticking out of the charred and blackened beams. Many of these were gathered up, silver plated and made into crosses. The largest of these crosses was set on an altar in the ruins; behind it stood a great charred cross of wood and behind that again, carved on the wall, the words 'Father Forgive'. Many little crosses of nails were sent to churches in all corners of the world, including Russia and East Berlin. The Coventry Cross of Nails had become a symbol of forgiveness, new life coming out of death, and reconciliation between people and nations.

In 1960 Canon Buchan, Rural Dean of Coventry, had suggested the idea that the Cross of Nails from the altar in the ruins of the old Cathedral should be carried round the diocese, from parish to parish, just before the consecration of the new Cathedral. The idea was taken up and developed. We planned a pilgrimage, to last forty days and forty nights, during which there should be kept a continuous chain of prayer. Each parish where the Cross rested should be a link in that chain and while they prayed for the diocese, the whole diocese should at that moment pray for them. The Cross would set out from the ruins on Palm Sunday, the day after the

Bishop's mission ended, and would return on 25th May, the eve of the consecration, and be set in the centre of the great gold cross on the altar of the new Cathedral. There it would stand with all its old significance, and in addition now as the symbol in the Mother Church of the love and prayer and unity of the diocese.

The story of those forty days and forty nights can be told by the diocese itself in words written under the impact of the experience. The following quotations were taken from parish magazines and from letters written to the Bishop.

Here, first of all, is a description of the Cross being handed over from one parish to another in Kenilworth, at 3 am:

In the distance we could discern the approach of the vicar of St John's carrying the Cross of Nails, and followed by his contingent with torches, and with three banners bearing the words 'A Diocese Prays', 'A Consecrated Cathedral demands a Consecrated People' and 'Father Forgive'. There was a sense of oneness and brotherhood in the hearts of every one of us as we saw them approach. Here was the Church of England passing on its message from parish to parish through the diocese. 'High' church or 'low' church didn't enter into it; this remarkable feature of unity in diversity that is characteristic of our Church was being demonstrated.

The two groups met and the ceremony of 'handing over' was begun. 'Receive this Cross of Nails, brought to you with the love and prayers of your fellows from the ruined sanctuary of our Cathedral Church of St Michael. Cherish this Cross, as a token of the merciful forgiveness of God, declared to us in the Passion of our saviour Jesus Christ. Watch about this Cross, in prayer for one another and for us, for Cuthbert our Bishop, and for all in this Diocese of Coventry who love and serve the Lord Jesus.'

Such were the words accompanying the handing over. Then, as the Cross was delivered into the hand of the priest of the receiving company, the first priest said in a loud voice 'CHRIST REIGNS'.

Then followed the prayer: 'Almighty God … grant that we walking in the way of the cross, may find it none other than the way of life and peace.'

This was followed by silence. The Cross was raised aloft. St John's returned to their church and we took the Cross further on its pilgrimage.

This scene was repeated over 100 times, by day and by night, in country lanes and city streets. Once the Cross travelled by water:

The Cross of Nails arrived in Stockingford at 10.30 pm on the Wednesday in Holy Week. It came by canal barge. The Stockingford contingent of about seventy people, with processional Cross raised and twelve torches flaring, waited on the puddle-strewn ground of the recreation ground by the side of the canal, and the barges, manned by sea scouts, drew alongside with whistles blaring.

The next day the Cross was at Atherstone. The vicar writes:

It is difficult to convey adequately just what it meant to people. They had a sense that they were taking part in history as they gathered at the brook in Church Walk, the ancient boundary between Mancetter and Atherstone, at 9 pm on Maundy Thursday night. Besides the 200 from St Mary's formed up round the banners of the different church organisations, many others had also collected there, including a man in a Salvation Army uniform. The small flickering lights of the torches growing larger in the darkness warned us of the approach of the Cross of Nails, and soon the short handing over ceremony was taking place.

The procession of 200, headed by the robed choir and the Cross of Nails carried alternately by the four wardens, went along the ancient Church Walk to the Watling Street. Motorists from north and south stopped and watched in curious silence, as well as people in the streets and the windows. At Church Street the procession, now swollen in numbers, turned off towards the marketplace to the parish church.

Inside, a few older people, unable to walk in the procession, were already in their places as the Cross was taken to the altar. The service of Holy Communion was soon under way. 150 of the 200 in church received communion. Many more than had promised stayed on into the hours of the night, praying round the Cross of Nails … At 1.30 am twenty-two men and three women bore the Cross and torches aloft and proceeded again down the Watling Street to the parish boundary. There we squashed ourselves into two minibuses and drove to Weddington. We disembarked and marched silently to hand over a little after 2 am, filling the small village church with our silent prayer for a while, before returning to our own parish and homes richer people.

On Good Friday night the Cross rested for an all-night vigil at Exhall and this was the pattern generally observed during the rest of the pilgrimage.

Churches that kept an all-night vigil reported again and again how people stayed for longer periods than they had promised. Praying seemed easy, as though they were caught up in a 'prayer better than their own prayers'.

The Bedworth congregation had formed a torchlight procession from their church. The advancing procession, singing hymns and outlined by the torches, was inspiring and unforgettable. Our congregation returned to Exhall, where the Cross remained on the altar throughout the night, and between 11 pm and 1 am there were about thirty people at prayer. This number decreased during the small hours, but was never less than ten. Although a rota of half-hours had been arranged, several stayed for longer periods of up to two hours.

On Easter Eve the Cross was at Bulkington:

The pilgrimage of the Cross of Nails and the reception in the parish was one of the most thrilling things that has happened to us … In a steady downpour of rain the procession started with about 100, chiefly men, and the choir with servers. Before we arrived at the parish church we were well over 250 … The service which followed was one of gratitude … There were never less than two dozen men and women in church while the Cross was on the high altar … We left the parish church to walk the two miles to the handover at Shilton. With lighted torches and thankful hearts the half hour passed too quickly. Every man in the procession carried the Cross of Nails, the general thought was that of honour, and a memory that will never be blotted out.

On Easter Day it passed through Brinklow:

The atmosphere in the church during those three hours of silent prayer was most impressive: it seemed alive with spiritual power. There were never less than about a dozen people in church, and at times more. Among these I noticed a row of 'chapel' people, and others whom I had not seen in church before … I think it is true to say that this pilgrimage of the Cross of Nails, and its accompanying chain of prayers, really stirred many people in this parish, and brought them close to God in real prayer. And the influence of this effort remains, as I find in talking to people. My personal impression is that this was more potent than the visit to the mission at Leamington.

So the Cross passed through towns and villages. Here is a comment from a Coventry housing estate, which received the Cross on a Sunday:

This made a tremendous impact upon the church and the parish … it was inspiring to see the church just crowded with eager people … The choir master, who has served under nine vicars, said, 'This is the most impressive and moving experience that I have ever witnessed.' A lady visitor from Yorkshire who serves in the educational world said, 'I have never been in such a service before in my life … I had been on unbroken duty from 7 am until after 8 pm, and one just forgot the physical weariness in the joy, inspiration and thrill of the experience.

And this from a village near Leamington:

A vigil was kept and parishioners constantly came into the church for silent prayer. At the end of the vigil the church was full, and a specially arranged Holy Communion service commenced. This was a most wonderful service – the whole church being caught up in a holy atmosphere too thrilling to describe.

But not all villages responded. This report comes from the vicar of two small parishes, a staunch Anglo-Catholic with a sense of humour.

Of the first parish he writes,

It was interesting to see people disappearing into their houses as the procession passed by! There must be some psychological explanation. There were at least two Methodists in the procession.

Of the second,

Many people came to their garden gates or to the foot of the branch roads to watch. Almost exactly the opposite reaction! I think there were two Roman Catholics in this procession.

Once at least the prayer was rudely interrupted:

A vigil was kept throughout the night. The first part of the vigil was kept by the church youth fellowship, but at the end of the stipulated period the quiet in the church was shattered by one of the choir boys bursting in and demanding brightly and loudly, 'Well, everybody feeling alright?'

On at least two occasions the Cross was carried round a hospital. At the Manor Hospital, Nuneaton:

A watch was kept in every ward, and the vicar spoke of the meaning of the Cross of Nails, and prayers were offered for all who suffer. Many prople of different backgrounds were looking at that Cross and asking all about it. Many patients had thought they would not be able to pray with the Cross of Nails because of their illness. It was a great joy to them that they could take part in hospital.

At the Central Hospital, Hatton:

> The chief male nurse asked that the Cross of Nails, on its pilgrimage through the parish, should be taken to the hospital chapel for a time, and the matron improved on this by suggesting that the patients and staff might meet the Cross at the hospital gate and walk with it in procession along the drive.

Once it visited a teachers' training college:

> At about midnight, the Cross left St Stephen's, Canley, to be handed over to the congregation of the parish church at Westwood in the centre of the City of Coventry Training College. The principal of the training college most happily allowed us to do this ... She and a good number of the staff with many of the students stayed up to witness the handover, and there were well over 120 out in the rain at 12.20 am.

Several times it was taken to the homes of people who were elderly or ill. Here is a description from Halford:

We made a personal call upon Miss Sutton and Miss Emett, who are ninety-six years and eighty-six years respectively. The school being next door, the children were all lined up outside, and we had a brief service of prayer and thanksgiving, with the old ladies joining in at their cottage window.

The same rector describes how the Cross left his parish:

We had the service of handing over the Cross, and my party waited for a while, watching the whole procession taking the Cross on its return journey to the Cathedral. As we stood watching, one of my young people said that it was a lovely sight, watching the Cross which he had helped to carry, going on its way. I think that was the feeling I had, an awe-inspiring feeling of gladness that an invisible bond had been created throughout the diocese. Perhaps I can better sum it up in the words of a parishioner when she said, 'Oh Rector, I am so glad to think we have had the Cross, and to pray for other people as well as for ourselves, and even though my feet are killing me, I would gladly walk with it again!'

He finishes his description with these words, which were echoed in other parts of the diocese:

Have we heard the end of it, or could this wonderful idea be given another chance next year? It would be very inspiring if this two-way flow of the Holy Spirit could be brought about again, the people to the Cross, and the Cross to the people. I am sure my parishes feel closer to their Mother Church now than ever before. This must never be lost. We shall pray for our Mother Church, and our Bishop, and all who minister and bear responsibility, knowing we shall not be forgotten by them.

We will finish with a few particular incidents and a general impression.

- It was a glorious morning and my churchwarden, a man of about seventy-four, born and bred in the parish, a member of the church all his life, remarked to me that this was 'the finest thing the church here has ever done'. This rather surprised me, because in recent days he had said there were too many things going on in the diocese and he didn't hold with it. However, this had caught his imagination, as it did with many unexpected people.

- The Cross bearer, David Shore, aged seventeen, and a post office telephone apprentice, had arranged a special day's leave to carry the cross on its journey through the parish.

- At 4 am, an old lady who is in her eighty-seventh year arrived and stayed until we left the church at 6.30.

- On this procession were a husband and wife who had recently parted after much domestic trouble. I could hardly believe my eyes when I saw them walking together in the procession.

- A parishioner was dying in a cottage near the route of the Cross of Nails. I had given him his communion, and shortly before the day of the visit, I had told him that the Cross of Nails was to arrive from Leamington early in the morning. As he was weak and in great pain and under drugs, I thought it best not to disturb him on the morning of the arrival of the Cross. When the procession came within sight, he was there at his bedroom window to see the procession file into church. After his death, his wife told me that by a great effort he had kept awake all through the night, afraid that he should fall asleep and not be there to see the Cross go into his own parish church.

And here is the general impression, repeated again and again in different words. The first two quotations are from towns, the last three from little villages.

- Without exception, everybody testified to the tremendous sense of spiritual presence and blessing through the night.

- Praying became less difficult and less of a struggle than it is sometimes, because those who prayed were aware of the deep and unseen fellowship of which the Cross of Nails was the symbol. The cross became a focal point of prayer. It captured the imagination of the people in a remarkable way. It is interesting to note that some who came to pray were only occasional worshippers themselves; they were drawn into a fellowship of prayer which became a converting experience.

- I looked in at intervals, but not during the last hour until about 9.40, when I was staggered to find quite fifty folk all quietly kneeling and waiting. I think one realised there and then something more of what is meant by 'atmosphere of prayer'.

- It was all very exciting, very impressive, and not a little mysterious, because I am quite sure that most of the people taking part had only the vaguest idea as to what it was all about, beyond being something to do with the consecration. However, I am equally certain that somehow they found that it had brought them a blessing.

- A quarter-hourly rota had been arranged. The vicar took his turn at 7–7.15 pm, and after handing over to his successor (a boy of sixteen) returned to the vicarage. At 8 pm, he returned to the church to be greeted by the most wonderful and impressive sight. The church was crowded with a larger number of people, all on their knees praying, than at many a normal Sunday service and the atmosphere in the parish church was quite indescribably beautiful and reverent. The vicar felt, in all humility, that the Holy Spirit had moved in a big way in his parish.

Chapter 7

Consecration

Three years ago we had begun to see that what God wanted was not just a consecrated Cathedral, but a consecrated people. So we planned that in the days before the consecration of the Cathedral, and if possible on the evening before, people all over the diocese should be given an opportunity to renew their Christian vows. Then, having offered ourselves to God, we might offer him a Cathedral.

For all of us, our Christian vows meant the vows we had taken at our baptism, when we were born again, and received into the family of Christ's church. For the clergy, it would mean also their ordination vows.

This led to a lot of heart-searching. Can these vows, taken once and for all, be renewed? We felt it better to say that we would *affirm* them; we would pledge our continuous loyalty to them, but now as people who were older and more experienced, and could understand their significance more deeply.

Then a further question arose. Should anyone be allowed just to walk in and affirm these solemn vows on the spur of the moment? We decided that lots of opportunities to prepare ourselves ought to be given, and that the services of affirmation would be better held at a special time on a weekday, so that people who had dropped into church casually on a Sunday should not find themselves caught up in doing something they knew nothing about. But we foresaw, rightly, that when it came to the point, nobody could presume to judge who was prepared and who was not prepared, and that each parish must be free to organise things in its own way.

To meet this problem as far as possible, and to help people affirm their vows with deeper understanding, Canon Patey produced a study outline on baptism for the winter of 1961–62. This was used up and down the diocese. One parish at least had discussion in place of the sermon: 'Our preparation centred round the three promises of our baptism, and at evening services we substituted a time of discussion, question and answer, in place of the normal sermon. Many people appreciated this opportunity of asking questions, and I feel sure that in the future we shall find this may well become a regular feature of our services.'

Meanwhile, the clergy were asked to prepare themselves to affirm the vows made at their ordination.

A little replica of the Cross of Nails was made, which could be given to each person after they had affirmed their vows, and pinned to a lapel. A special form of service was drawn up, which used words from the Methodist Covenant Service, setting them within the framework of the Holy Communion. We guessed that 10,000 copies of the service and crosses of nails should be sufficient.

But we had hopelessly underestimated. Caught up in the inspiration of those forty days and forty nights, people came in totally unexpected numbers. Sometimes vows were affirmed while the Cross of Nails was actually in the church, as on these two Coventry housing estates:

- The parish church was so full that a dozen stood throughout the service. At the daughter church we had the largest number of communicants ever to attend a service at 6.30 pm, on a Wednesday evening, in the presence of the Cross of Nails.

- At 3.30 pm the adults followed the Cross into the church for the first Affirmation Service. The church was packed. I expected moderate support, but nothing like this … At the Affirmation Service there was a woman who used to come to our church when it was first consecrated, but has not been for over two years; a young confirmation candidate who had not been for over two years; a mother whose baby is dying from leukaemia, but who brought her baby boy to a healing service the previous Sunday. About 185 people affirmed their baptismal vows … I have been tremendously impressed by this experience – the people making a witness in their own parish, the priest reminding himself and the congregation of his ordination vows, and the congregation praying for their priest as he knelt before them.

In one parish, the laity affirmed their vows in the presence of the Cross of Nails, and the clergy later:

On Sunday, at Evensong, came the affirmation of ordination vows. I discovered afterwards that at the same time as we were affirming our vows, the Bishop was affirming his consecration vows at the Cathedral. All of us have been doing it. It has been a period of humble dedication, which we pray we may be able to give greater substance to as the days wear on. Our preacher is a retired clergyman, now living in our parish. He joined us in the affirmation, and so did a Church Army Captain, as he renewed the promises made at his commissioning. The questions were put to us by a student reading for Holy Orders. Thus, there were what one might think of as three generations of the ministry replying to questions put by one who is yet to be ordained.

From one tiny country parish comes this comment:

> I was amazed and astounded at the response. No fewer than forty-eight made their communion at this service, and there were sixteen others besides them, making a total of sixty-four. I asked the communicants to remain kneeling after they had received communion, and to each I gave the small replica of the Cross of Nails. I then asked the others to come forward and kneel at the rail as they too received their replica. Incidentally, among these latter were two men who had never been to a service before and it is possible (but only possible at present) that one of those may come forward for confirmation. From discussions later, I have learned that this service of affirmation had an immense impact on those present – vastly more than the visit of the Cross of Nails. May I just add that it is my considered opinion that such a service held again some years from now – say five years – would have at least a similar, if not greater, impact. But I would also add that I think it essential that the service be held within the framework of Holy Communion.

Here is a similar thought from another village where the vicar had been ill:

> One event I know personally which was very splendid was the Affirmation Service on the eve of the consecration. Although my doctor told me not to attempt attendance at

the actual consecration, I did conduct the affirming service and it was a most wonderful experience and we were all very greatly moved. My feeling is that if at some further infrequent interval we could get our churchpeople to come forward voluntarily to affirm their belief and make a declaration openly before others, it would lead to a strengthening of real practical value to us all.

The form of the service was as follows: The priest reminded the people of the New Covenant which Jesus made with his disciples, and called upon us at this time of the consecration of our Cathedral to affirm our own vows of consecration, and joyfully and solemnly to renew the covenant which binds us to God. After the reading of the Gospel, in which Jesus repeats to us his New Commandment ('This is my commandment, that ye love one another, as I have loved you'), the priest called us to affirm our baptismal vows, to renounce Satan, to believe in God and to keep his commandments. Then the people sat and the priest affirmed the declaration made at his ordination, after which the people prayed for him:

Almighty God, who hath given you this
will to do all these things;
Grant also unto you strength and
power to perform the same;
That he may accomplish his work
which he hath begun in you;
Through Jesus Christ Our Lord, Amen.

Then all knelt together in silence. After a while the priest said, in the name of all:

O Lord God, Holy Father, who has called us through Christ to be partakers in this gracious covenant, we take upon ourselves with joy the yoke of obedience and engage ourselves, for love of thee, to seek and do thy perfect will. We are no longer our own, but thine.

Here all the people joined:

I am no longer my own, but thine. Put me to what thou wilt, rank me with whom thou wilt; put me to doing, put me to suffering; let me be employed for thee or laid aside for thee, exalted for thee or brought low for thee; let me be full, let me be empty; let me have all things, let me have nothing; I freely and heartily yield all things to thy pleasure and disposal.

And now, O Glorious and blessed God, Father, Son and Holy Spirit, thou art mine and I am thine. So be it. And the covenant which I have made on earth, let it be ratified in heaven. Amen.

Then followed the Holy Communion, for how could we keep such promises in our own strength? We knew that within a few days, if not a few hours, we should all have betrayed our vows of consecration. So we came back to that moment when Jesus consecrated himself, and from which he gives us again and again down the ages his consecrated body and blood.

Who, in the same night that he was betrayed, took bread; and when he had given thanks, he brake it, and gave it to his disciples, saying, Take, eat, this is my body which is given for you … likewise the cup … this is my blood of the New Covenant, which is shed for you and for many for the remission of sins: Do this, as oft as ye shall drink it, in remembrance of me.

On the night of 24th May 1962 this service was held in many parish churches up and down Warwickshire, and in the city of Coventry itself. There, in St John's Church, at the opposite end of the shopping precinct to the Cathedral, the Cross of Nails was resting for the last hours of its pilgrimage and the last link in the long chain of prayer. As the service of Holy Communion ended, the Cross was carried out of the church to where the Bishop was waiting to receive it, accompanied by a great crowd from the other city churches. He himself, as Father of the whole family, carried the cross on that last stage of the journey back to the Mother Church. The procession could hardly push its way through the crowds that had gathered in the precinct, and when the Bishop reached the ruins of the old Cathedral, where the cross had stood for so many years, he found it packed with people from wall to wall. There the Cross was handed back to the Provost and carried into the new Cathedral to be set in position above the high altar at the centre of the diocese, the symbol of love, forgiveness, prayer and unity. During that last night before the consecration, a vigil of prayer was kept by members of the Cathedral congregation.

It is not my place to describe in this book 25th May 1962, the day we had prepared for so eagerly, and which so gloriously surpassed our every hope. Certain moments live in the memory – the entrance of the Queen, the Bishop crying, 'Open the doors', the moment of the consecration itself when with drums rolling and a fanfare of trumpets the choirs sang Alleluia! Alleluia! Alleluia! and the congregation burst into a hymn of praise. But without doubt the greatest moment of all came the next morning, when the consecration of the Cathedral was completed by the celebrating within it of the Holy Communion. Then the Bishop stood at the heart of his diocese, and taking a little loaf of bread in his hands, he repeated the agelong words:

> Who, in the same night that he was betrayed, took bread, and when he had given thanks, he brake it, and gave it to his disciples.

As the prayer ended, the trumpets sounded, and there followed a profound silence.

During the next three weeks we experienced an extraordinary outburst of worship and happiness as the whole diocese celebrated a festival from end to end. Great services were held in the new Cathedral, offering up to God every part of our daily lives. There were services for industry and agriculture, for schools, for local government, the armed forces, youth, old age pensioners and the medical services, to mention only a few. There was a Service of International Reconciliation, when young people of many nations asked the burning questions that confront the world today, and when churchpeople from many countries and denominations moved together into the chancel, and kneeling before the great tapestry of Christ reigning in glory, prayed for his forgiveness and for the coming of his kingdom.

Many of these acts of worship were made by artists. There was the first performance of Benjamin Britten's *War Requiem*, that work of unbelievable power and beauty and insight, where the futility of war is set against the eternal mercy of God. Sung under the compassionate gaze of the Christ who looks down from Graham Sutherland's tapestry, it summed up and expressed the whole meaning of the Cathedral with a poignancy that was almost intolerable. After the service Sir Basil Spence, the architect, and Benjamin Britten, the composer, met, and, both deeply moved, thanked one another for the music and the Cathedral. Through the inspiration of those two men and the travail of all their fellow artists who had built and adorned the Cathedral and sung and played the music, God's truth had come to birth and been spoken that night, and we who had seen and heard 'rejoiced with an exceeding great joy'. Many of the artists who performed in the Cathedral during those weeks were caught up in the worship. Yehudi Menuhin, standing alone in the chancel, seemed almost to shine and become transfigured and to be one with his violin and with the music which poured out of him. Edric Connor, going up to sing, whispered 'pray for me', and then sang with such electrifying power of Jesus rescuing someone from hell that 2,000 people gripped their chairs in terror and relief, and he himself returned to his seat trembling and pouring with sweat.

This did not only happen inside the Cathedral. Two visitors from London and Exeter experienced the same infectious and liberating power as they addressed a meeting in a church hall:

> I spoke to these people from the other end of the diocese from the new Cathedral as I did not know I could speak. All trace of nervousness left me – I had wanted to be sick the minute before – but now knew just what I must say, and said it simply and clearly. The Archdeacon of Exeter spoke next – and he speaks very wonderfully – but I have never heard such beauty of words and depth of spirit from him before, and very rarely indeed from anyone ... We had seen a glimpse of the beginnings of the Church, a sanctified people one in Christ. Only the beginnings, as they them-

selves would be the first to say. How great the glory; how precious the treasure of grace; how feeble our love. I, too, you see, was being consecrated.[1]

Finally, some words that were written at the end of the festival of consecration:

These are the outward events, but those of us who have passed through them know that we have experienced the Holy Spirit.

Let me hasten to say, this experience has not been hysterical. A young woman in a remote village felt it, and she said to me, 'This is more wonderful than the Billy Graham campaign. Then we were worked up. Now we are relaxed and happy.'

Perhaps we have come to know a tiny bit of what Jesus meant when he said, 'I will send you the Spirit of truth'. We have seen reality break through, like the sun through a fog, sweeping away the pretences. People have been set free, to become what they really are. We have begun to know that a whole diocese could be a fellowship of the Holy Spirit. We have begun to hear the Spirit speaking to us through artists, and through men and women outside the official Church.

Someone said to me the other day, 'What a relief when we can get back to normal!' I know what he means: we cannot live forever on a mountain top. But God forbid that we should ever get back to that sub-normal state, that twilight of unreality and suspicion, shut off from the Spirit of truth. We know, now, that when men and women make themselves available to God together, in love and prayer, then the Spirit who is already within them can break out and take control. These are the three who dance together and are one at the heart of the Church – Love, Prayer, the Holy Spirit. All else is secondary.[2]

1   J.S.F. Parker, *Parish Magazine of St Augustine's*, Highgate, July 1962.

2   *Church Times*, July 27 1962.

PART TWO

The Meaning

A NEW
COMMANDMENT
I GIVE UNTO YOU +
THAT YE LOVE
ONE ANOTHER AS
I HAVE LOVED YOU

Chapter 8

The New Commandment

The first part of this book is the story of what happened and I believe that through the story God has spoken. So in the second part we shall try to see the pattern of the story as a whole, and to draw out its meaning.

Three years before the consecration of the Cathedral we had begun to see that 'a consecrated Cathedral demands a consecrated people'. Rather nervously we had asked, 'What does it mean to be a consecrated people? And what, O Lord God who created the universe, do You want *us* to do *now?*'

'One question at a time,' replied God, 'and let us begin with the second. I command you, now, to love one another with the love of Jesus. Then to pray together in the name of Jesus. The meaning will be revealed to you later.'

As we had begun to explore that love, climbing off our pedestals and out of our entrenched positions, meeting one another, listening, learning – as we had groped together towards a united prayer around the Cross – God had revealed to us the meaning of consecration. The Holy Spirit had grasped hold of us. We had begun to know a fire of love burning inside us, and a rushing mighty wind of prayer blowing through our towns and villages.

Of course, the Holy Spirit is always blowing through the Church. That is the continuous miracle down the generations, that through the Church, with all her obvious failings, there still blows the wind of the love of Jesus. But how gently it blows. We sing a hymn about the Holy Spirit:

> And his that gentle voice we hear
> Soft as the breath of even.

We know him as an evening breeze just rustling the leaves, not as a force 7 gale, in which 'whole trees are in motion and inconvenience is felt when walking against the wind'.[1]

The reason is that we do not obey the New Commandment – that, at any rate, is what this story suggests. Of course, we obey it up to a point, and one can find in every place little groups of Christians who love one another. But on the whole, this is not the image the Church presents to the world.

I remember when I first read a paper called *Theology*. It was out in Egypt in 1943 and a kind aunt sent me a copy. I was amazed at the hatred which boiled and spat out of its pages, as Christians engaged in controversy with one another. My job, at the time, was propaganda against the enemy, but these Christians outdid in bitterness towards each other anything we could think up against the Germans. If you read the correspondence column of the *Church Times*, you will be struck most weeks by this same bitterness. When I was ordained, I expected that I should find myself in a new atmosphere, where people loved one another. It was a shock to discover that this was not so. Individually, most clergy are humble people who work long hours in the service of their parishioners. But we do not, on the whole, love one another, any more than, for example, doctors or schoolteachers. There is a barrier of shyness and artificiality between clergy and laity, and all too often we fail to break it down and enter into a Christian fellowship where we accept one another as real people. In our parishes there is too often jealousy of other parishes, suspicion of 'them' at the centre of the diocese and hostility to the theologians and other 'bright sparks' of the Church with their newfangled ideas.

All this is terrifyingly like the world around us and unlike Jesus, and is the main cause of the church's failure to attract. For though we preach the gospel in challenging sermons, though we have deep insight into social problems and a clear grasp of the kingdom faith, though we have successful Christian stewardship and live lives of great personal self-sacrifice, yet, if we do not love one another, all this is empty noise, and worth nothing. St Paul said it long ago, 'Though I speak with the tongues of men and of angels and have not charity, I am become as sounding brass, or a tinkling cymbal … though I give my body to be burned and have not charity, it profiteth me nothing' (1 Corinthians 13:1–3). The reason all this activity is empty noise and worth nothing, is that God is not in it. St John tells us that the man who does not love his brother is not God's child (1 John 3:10). He says again, 'If a man say "I love God", while hating his brother, he is a liar' (1 John 4:20).

The prime duty of the Christian Church, therefore, is to obey the New Command-ment. We must understand what it is, and reorganise ourselves to obey it.

First, we must understand what it is. It is *new*. It is not just a command to love one another. This had been said before Jesus lived, for example by a Jewish writer in the *Testament of the Twelve Patriarchs*, written at least one hundred years before Christ:

> Love ye each one his brother, and put away hatred from your hearts; love one another in deed, and in word, and in the inclination of the soul … Love one another, and with long-suffering hide ye one another's faults. For God delighteth in the unity of brethren … And if any one seeketh to do evil

unto you, do well unto him, and pray for him, and ye shall be redeemed of the Lord from all evil.

But we are now commanded '*as I have loved you,* so you are to love one another'. This is what makes it *new*. Jesus gave the commandment just after he had washed his friends' dirty, stinking, ugly feet. You must love like that, with a love that is humble, costly, that comes alongside people just as they are, and is ready to serve them. At that same supper he took bread, and broke it, and gave it to them, and said, 'this is my body given for you'. You must love like that, with a love that is generous, self-giving, prepared to be broken. Indeed, if we would really know what kind of love it is, we must look to the moment when he was actually broken, to Jesus hanging on the cross in the darkness, as he cried that terrible and lonely cry, 'My God, My God, why hast thou forsaken me?' Here is a love that embraces me just as I am, that accepts me in all the repulsiveness of my sin, a love that is made sin for my sake and for my sake cut off from God. I must love like that, with a love that utterly identifies itself with all ugly and perverted and lost people and stands on their side against the world, and shares their darkness and their suffering.

Because we cannot do that, because it is far out of our reach, Jesus gave us a *commandment*. He did not invite us or encourage us to be kind to people. He commanded us to love with a love like his, long after we feel like it, even when the person we must love is repulsive to us.

So it is both *new*, and a *commandment*. These two things are important for us to understand, for it is only because Jesus has done it first, and then because he commands us to follow his example, that it becomes possible for us to obey.

But having understood, we must reorganise ourselves to obey; and what we need chiefly is *time*. This springs out of the story in

Part One. When the clergy of the Monks Kirby Chapter were invited to meet weekly, they laughed, for they knew they hadn't got time. They were far too busy. They were so busy doing things that matter very much that they had no time for the thing which matters most of all.

The thing which matters most of all is to love the people closest to you and for most of us this means our families. Very often both clergy and lay people are so busy with church work that they have to neglect their families and in so doing they undermine all their work for God. This was brought home to me vividly one afternoon after I had been working flat out for six years as vicar on a new housing estate. I went for a walk with my wife and children, pushing the pram, and one of my parishioners looked over his garden hedge in astonishment. 'That's the best thing you've done for me in six years,' he said.

The furious activity of clergy and lay people is something to be hated, opposed and laughed at, as being of the very devil. Most of us are afraid of being found doing nothing, lest people should think we were idle. But a wise man once told me, 'Your priorities must be first prayer, second rest, and third work.' When you have established your times of prayer and your times of rest, you can give what time remains to work.

This means, from my own experience, that married clergy must have:

- every day at least two hours to devote to their home
- every week at least a full day off
- every year at least four clear weeks; the churchwardens must make sure the clergy can afford to get away and bully them if they won't.

People in other professions must be equally firm to ensure that they themselves get proper rest.

Having made time for our families, we must make time for the fellow Christians who are closest to us. This again springs directly out of the story in Part One. For clergy, this means a weekly meeting of the chapter. I speak from vivid experience over the last four years, during which a group of us have met every Monday morning. We have prayed, studied the Bible, and discussed our work together and this meeting has come for us all to be the most important engagement of the week. Here we have time to meet and to listen to God speaking through the Bible and through one another. We have come to know one another intimately and to see through the mask into the real person behind it. We have come to know one another's weaknesses and to love each other because of them. We are people of very different temperaments and often we argue fiercely. Only a week or two ago my tallest colleague stood over me with clenched fists and flashing eyes and shouted, 'I utterly repudiate everything you say.' But we can afford to argue, for we know that each is genuine, and really believes what they say in an honest heart. We know that each of the others has something to teach us and that we shall only reach the truth if we allow everybody to make their contribution. Above all, we know that only as a close-knit team can we do the work that God has given us to do.

But this does not only apply to clergy. In chapter 4 we saw a group of lay people coming to this same experience, and one member of the group saying, 'You can go on for too long being an ordinary member of a parish without being challenged personally. And what we found ourselves being challenged to do was not necessarily in the parish, but to do things with our lives. Not to be *busy*, but to convert our lives, to turn to more kindly thoughts and things like that.'

Two immensely important truths spring out of that comment. First, that the average congregation is too big for people really to meet one another. For years you may attend church and parish functions, but never come to this painful and dangerous meeting with another Christian. Secondly, that being busy is often an escape from this deep meeting with other people, in which they are going to see my weaknesses and I am going to discover my own.

But such meeting, with a small group of between eight and twelve people, is what Christians need if they are fully to discover themselves and to discover Christ. This insight is nothing new. It has been breaking out of the Church of England ever since the Reformation. Wesley made it one of the methods of Methodism. In the last twenty years there has grown up within the Church of England a movement called Servants of Christ the King, which one can only join by becoming a member of a 'company'. Each company consists of about eight to twelve people and makes its own rule of life and discovers its own 'object' towards which God is calling it. There are over 100 of these companies up and down the country and the overall object of every one of them is to 'wait upon God together'. Their technique for doing this properly belongs to the next chapter, but here it must be said that in these little cells, deeply involved with one another, many Christians have woken up to a more abundant kind of life which can only be called the fellowship of the Holy Spirit.

This chapter must end by meeting an objection that is always raised. 'You are telling us to form pious cliques, inward-looking, concerned with themselves and not with the world. This is surely the opposite of what Jesus intended. He sent his disciples out to convert the world.' Others throw doubt on the New Commandment itself and suggest that at this point St John's Gospel is at its weakest. The true voice of Jesus is not to be heard commanding the disciples to love one another, but to go out and love and save sinners.

To the first objection the behaviour of Jesus is itself the answer. He formed a 'clique', if that is what you want to call it. It consisted of twelve *apostles*, which means people 'sent out'. But before they could be sent out, they had to be with Jesus, and with one another. They were men of varied temperaments, education and political views and they often quarrelled and jostled one another for position. But Jesus formed such a little company round him because he knew that this is the right number of people to learn the truth about God together. You do not learn it best alone. You do not learn it best in a great crowd. You learn it best where twelve people are gathered round Jesus. Whatever else the pattern of the Church ought to include, surely we are mad to exclude the one pattern which Our Lord himself instituted! We might further notice that within the 'clique' of twelve, Jesus had an inner 'clique' of three, Peter, James and John, and if we are to believe St John himself, within the 'clique' of three he had one disciple whom he particularly loved.

It was this disciple whom he particularly loved who has given us the New Commandment. For he above all men had learnt that out of deep love springs the Holy Spirit. And here we discover the secret of why the New Commandment is the very foundation on which the kingdom of God is built – because out of obedience to the New Commandment springs the fire of love and the wind of prayer which is the Holy Spirit.

The Church is often likened to a boat. We Christians are like people rowing that boat, frantically busy, strained, panting, exhausted. But all the time the wind is blowing, and if only we would hoist the sail, the boat would move much faster, driven by a power far greater than we can generate ourselves. Then we should no more be straining, but sitting alert at the tiller, feeling the kick of the waves and the tug of the wind, every nerve and muscle concentrated on keeping the boat from overturning, and holding her on her true course.

This began to happen in the Coventry Diocese in 1962. It could happen anywhere if we would hoist the sail of a company of Christians who obeyed the New Commandment. If they had the courage to love one another with the love of Jesus, they would be swept out into the world by the Holy Spirit to love and save sinners in his name.

---

1   It is significant that this hymn has been emasculated in
    Hymns Ancient and Modern. The verse has been cut out which says,
          He came in tongues of living flame
          To teach, convince, subdue
          All powerful as the wind he came.

Chapter 9

The New Prayer

Try to obey the New Commandment and you will find that you cannot. There is nothing so powerful in all the world to bring you to prayer.

This again springs out of the story in Part One. Groups of people all over the diocese came to a new experience of Christian fellowship, but when in the security of that fellowship they saw who they really were, and the terrifying work of love to which God was calling them, they came to know their need of God as never before.

Here is a description of a group at work. It is written by a laywoman, and dated Leamington Spa, 14th October 1961:

> I think we all and each of us went to the first meeting think-ing, 'All these other people are so clever and deeply religious, so why include me?' But that first meeting was spent getting to know each other and we soon found out that we were all just learners and seekers after truth. We even discovered that the clergy are not surpliced saints. They are humble seekers just like us. What astonished me was the fact that doubts and fears and joys which I had thought were my own particular quirks were common property, shared by other

people … At first we were a bit shy and diffident about speaking, but we soon thawed. We read Bible passages and discussed their application to our own lives and to parochial life. We learnt to pray together. We learnt to pray seated in each other's drawing rooms. We learnt to pray extemporarily. I must confess that I find the kind of praying that we do silently in the Lady Chapel on Thursday mornings much easier, but we learnt to respect each other's tastes.

And that brings me to our reactions to these meetings. Three things stand out very clearly …

First, that we have developed a great feeling of Christian fellowship. The kind of fellowship that caused observers of the early church to exclaim, without sarcasm, 'How these Christians love one another.'

Secondly, that we have become acutely aware of the power of prayer and of the need for every aspect of life, personal and parochial, to be rooted and grounded in prayer.

Thirdly, we have become aware that there is a priesthood of the laity. That is, that the laity as well as the clergy are called to the task of evangelism.

One of us says that this year has been a course of shock treatment. I myself was driven to go into retreat by the feeling that was common to many of us, that one must put one's own house in order before one can hope to pass on the challenge.

So we come to the question, what exactly is this challenge?

I believe it is putting ourselves utterly and completely at God's disposal. I do not believe that this is a question of a Billy Graham 'decision for Christ'. I think it goes far deeper than that. I think it is a process of self-surrender, that may take a lifetime to accomplish. I think it is a terrifying idea. It may lead one anywhere to the outposts of the mission field, to evangelism in Coventry's factories, to a life of prayer in a nunnery. It is a matter of faith. Can I really trust God not only to order my life by his governance, but to supply the grace and power that I may faithfully fulfil his will?

This lady is writing out of the heat and heart of the experience, and she emphasises two things:

- 'We learnt to pray together.'
- The challenge is 'putting ourselves utterly and completely at God's disposal'.

Praying together

This, I believe, is the missing factor in most Christian prayer, that we do not really pray together. We may be kneeling in the same church at the same time, but not as people between whom the barriers are down and who love one another with the love of Jesus. This is what began to happen, in an elementary form, in the Coventry Diocese during those years. Groups of clergy went away for a whole day to be silent together; clergy and laity met week after week, and came to understand one another more deeply. Then in the forty days and forty nights of prayer during the pilgrimage of the Cross of Nails a whole diocese was linked together and open to one another, and as we began to obey the New Commandment, so we began to experience the New Prayer.

At God's disposal

This is the keynote of the New Prayer. When that Monks Kirby Chapter went away together for a quiet day, right at the beginning of the story, they put themselves at God's disposal. They asked him, 'What do you want us to do?' They listened to the Bible, to one another, and to the silence, expecting an answer. They didn't just say, in a vague and general sort of way 'Thy will be done', but they asked, 'what in particular, O Lord God who created the universe, do you want *us* to do *now*?' They discovered, as did many other groups later, that what God wanted was not so much that they should *do* anything, as that they should *become* something. They were asked to surrender their pride.

Prayer of this kind, that is, companies of Christians putting themselves together at the disposal of God, has been springing out of the Church all down the centuries. We can see it very clearly in the Society of Friends (the Quakers). Their very name emphasises the first element, that they are praying together as men and women who love one another, and their method of prayer and of doing business is simply to put themselves at the disposal of God. A meeting for worship consists of silence, during which all listen together for God's word, and out of which anyone may speak as the Spirit moves them. It is remarkable how often the Spirit does in fact speak through first one and then another, so that by the end of the hour he has led the group as a whole 'into all truth'. When Friends meet for business, the 'concern' for which they have met is first laid before them, and then considered in silence. After a while, any who wish may speak and the chair will then sum up the 'sense of the meeting', and a unanimous decision is taken. If a decision is not unanimous there will be further silence and discussion until agreement is reached.

Within the Church of England, the Servants of Christ the King have adopted a very similar method. Their name emphasises the second element of prayer, that they are at Christ's disposal, but their whole organisation emphasises the first element of togeth-erness, since every member must belong to a company. The purpose of every company meeting is to 'wait upon God.' Again, the subject under discussion is outlined and then considered in silence. After the silence, each member is invited to speak in turn and if someone wishes to speak nobody must interrupt them till they have finished. At the end, the leader sums up the sense of the meeting and a unanimous decision is taken. Here again, the company comes to know God's will through giving full weight to the contribution of each member.

Part of the discipline of such a group seems to be that they should pray daily for each other. I know of one little group of eight people who have been meeting for over three years. They pray daily for three causes, for those who are suffering, for Christian unity, and for the Provost of our Cathedral. But their fourth object, which is essential to the other three, is to pray daily for each other. For this means that every morning, as they pray in their separate homes, they do so not as individuals, but as members of a company who love one another. They only meet once a month, to celebrate the Holy Communion together, but every day they are 'together at Christ's disposal'. Several groups of the same kind have recently sprung up in a Coventry housing-estate parish. They are known as 'the twelves' and their object is to make contact with their neighbours who are living outside the Church. They only meet once a fortnight, but again their discipline is to pray daily for each other.

It may be that we need such small groups, where we become deeply involved with one another, in order that we may know at its fullest power the New Prayer, which is prayer in the name of Jesus. For he himself seems to have felt the need of his own little prayer group of Peter, James and John, whom he took with him when he went to raise Jairus' daughter from the dead, and again to the Mount of Transfiguration and the Garden of Gethsemane, which were the beginning and the end of his own journey to the cross. At those moments he put himself utterly at the disposal of God. He became transparent so that the glory of God shone through him, and he became empty of all self-will, so that the power and love of God could flow through him to heal and save the world. But at those very moments he needed his friends to be linked with him in prayer. On that night of the last supper it is for the disciples he prays, 'I pray for them; I am not praying for the world, but for those whom Thou hast given Me' (John 17:9). And especially for Simon Peter, 'Simon, Simon, take heed: Satan has been given leave to sift all of you like wheat; but for you I have prayed that your faith may not fail; and when you have come to yourself you must lend strength to your brothers' (Luke 22:31). When he came to the Garden of Gethsemane, he urgently needed that they should pray with him. 'He took Peter and James and John with him. Horror and dismay came over him and he said to them, "My heart is ready to break with grief; stop here and stay awake." Then he went forward a little, threw himself on the ground, and prayed that, if it were possible, this hour might pass him by. "Abba, Father," he said, "all things are possible to Thee; take this cup away from me. Yet not what I will but what Thou wilt"' (Mark 14:33–36).

Here is both an utter self-abandonment to the will of God, and also a naked, agonizing dependence on his friends to share that prayer with him. That is what prayer in the name of Jesus is going to involve…

And now comes the surprise, the reward, the miracle. If we will have the courage to pray and to go on praying like that, needing God and needing one another in all humility, then we shall 'receive the Holy Ghost'. The Spirit of prayer himself will lay hold of us, and leap up out of our hearts.

This is what our story shows – as the Cross of Nails passed from parish to parish it was not so much we who prayed prayer, as prayer who prayed us. From deep down inside us there sprang a river of prayer – just exactly as Jesus had promised that it would.

'"Streams of living water shall flow out from within him." He was speaking of the Spirit which believers in him would receive later' (John 7:38–39). This is the experience of prayer that St Paul describes in the life of the early Christians, 'The Spirit you have received is … a Spirit that makes us sons, enabling us to cry "Abba, Father!"' And again, 'The Spirit comes to the aid of our weakness. We do not even know how we ought to pray, but through our inarticulate groans, the Spirit himself is pleading for us' (Romans 8:15–16). In other words, prayer is the Holy Spirit praying from within us.

This, I believe, is the New Prayer, or prayer in the name of Jesus. It is not reserved for specialists and mystics who can climb up a ladder of perfection, but it is gladly given by God to all humble Christians who will love their fellow Christians and put themselves at God's disposal. This again is what Jesus has promised in the simplest possible language: 'Where two or three have met together in my name,' he said, 'there am I in the midst' (Matthew 18:20). And after he had given the disciples the 'Our Father', he made a wonderful and encouraging comment on it. He told them that if they would persevere in such prayer, they would be given the Holy Spirit. 'If you then, bad as you are, know how to give your children what is good for them, how much more will the heavenly Father give the Holy Spirit to those who ask (and go on asking) him' (Luke 11:13).

The only condition is that we should persevere, for the Holy Spirit is not given to us until we have done all in our power, and reach the limit of our endurance, and come to that moment of helplessness and humility in which we are ready to accept God's gift. Then we discover that there was indeed a ladder of perfection to be climbed:

The perfect picture that St Teresa of Lisieux has drawn of the spiritual life will help to give us courage. She sees it as a stairway to be climbed, at the top of which God is waiting, looking down in Fatherly love at his child's efforts to surmount the first step. The child, who represents ourselves, fails to manage to climb even the first step; it can only keep on lifting up its tiny little foot. Sooner or later God takes pity on it, and comes down and sweeps the child right up to the top in his arms; but – and St Teresa insists on this as much as she insists on God's loving kindness – we must keep on lifting the foot … It seems to be a law of the spiritual life that, since all progress ultimately depends on God, he lets us first learn our complete helplessness by long and weary efforts that come to naught. But we have his word: 'I myself will come and save you!'[1]

---

1   M.E. Boylan, *Difficulties in mental prayer*, chapter 9.

Chapter 10

The New Gift

If we will obey the New Commandment and persevere with the New Prayer, then God will give us the Holy Spirit.

This chapter must be written in honour of Our Lord the Holy Spirit, and the first thing to say in his praise is that he cannot be grasped by us, but we must be grasped by him. He cannot be caught and put in a pot and the lid fastened down on him, for he is like fire and wind and flowing water. If you shut up fire in a pot it goes out; if you shut up wind in a pot it becomes still and stale; if you shut up flowing water in a pot it becomes stagnant. So you cannot trap the Spirit in any form or pattern of ecclesiastical organisation. Even though your pot be the Holy Catholic Apostolic Church itself, you cannot shut up Our Lord the Holy Spirit inside it. Nor can you contain him in words and shut him up within the chapter of a book; the best one may hope for is to describe him in action as he passes, 'That's the Holy Spirit – that was!'

What we discovered about him was, first of all, that he is the Spirit of love and the Spirit of prayer. When people begin to love one another with the love of Jesus, they are grasped by a love greater than their own love and when they begin praying together in the name of Jesus, they are invaded by a prayer more powerful than their own prayer.

This is something natural and obvious and within the experience of us all. When a team plays football, and they really play together, trusting one another and without jealousy but with a common eagerness to win, then they are invaded by a team spirit which carries them to victories otherwise beyond their reach. When a family goes on holiday together and father and mother have time to get to know one another all over again and to eat and explore and play games with the children, then they are invaded by a family spirit which brings them an infectious happiness deeper and richer than that of ordinary life. So it is with Christians, who are also a team and a family. Only they are centred not upon a football or a dinner table, but upon Jesus, and if they will be open to one another and to him what they come to experience is the Spirit of Jesus, or *Holy* Spirit. The Holy Spirit stamps upon them the two hallmarks of the character of Jesus himself, love and prayer. But he does more than this. He makes them not only his dwelling place, but the channel through which he can flow to others. Through their little love comes the love of Jesus and through their feeble prayer comes the prayer of Jesus. Welling up from within, the Holy Spirit of love and prayer fills them and overflows into the world with victorious power and infectious happiness.

But we also discovered that he was the Spirit of truth. This again arises directly out of the story in Part One and is exactly what Jesus promised: 'When he comes, who is the Spirit of truth, he will guide you into all truth' (John 16:13).

We experienced the Spirit of truth in a multitude of ways. First, as the inner voice that tells us what to do. Away back before our story started at all, the original question had been, 'What is the Spirit saying to the churches?' This is the right question for Christians to ask, for if you do ask it, you are likely to hear the Spirit guiding you, and if you do not ask it you are very unlikely to hear him.

May I illustrate this all-important point from a nursery rhyme?

Pussy Cat, Pussy Cat, where have you been?
I've been up to London to look at the Queen.
Pussy Cat, Pussy Cat, what saw you there?
I saw a little mouse, under her chair.

This cat was not interested in queens. A cat *may* look at a queen, but very rarely does, for it is far more interested in mice. So this cat saw what it was really interested in and heard the answer to the question it was really asking. In the same way a Christian *may* look to and listen for Our Lord the Holy Spirit, but very rarely does so. The Christian is too busy and interested in church mice and inevitably gets the answer to the question he or she really asks. (This criticism is at any rate true of myself, though it may not apply to anyone else.)

Once the right question is asked, 'What is the Spirit saying to the churches?' then the possibility is open for the Spirit of truth to speak to us and lead us into all truth. This he began to do immediately, and his truth was unfolded to us step by step. The clergy were told to go away together and be quiet and pray and wait upon God; out of this listening they were told to meet regularly and the challenge of the New Commandment was presented to them.

Then we began to experience the Spirit of truth in a second way, as the one who is 'the leader of the group', the inner voice not so much of the individual as of the company. In so far as we learnt to listen to one another, we found that the truth of God was springing out of the heart of a company of friends. As we relaxed and studied the Bible together and allowed each one to contribute the truth they understood, every one of us, both clergy and lay, was lifted up by the Spirit into a fuller understanding. Love led us into truth and St Paul's prayer was answered in our own experience, 'that he may grant you strength and power through his Spirit in your inner being, that through faith Christ may dwell in your hearts in love. With deep roots and firm foundations, may you be strong to grasp, with all God's people, what is the breadth and length and height and depth of the love of Christ, and to know it, though it is beyond knowledge' (Ephesians 3:16–18).

It was exhilarating to be learning new truth in a company of friends, but also very painful. Most of us resist new truth through arrogance and fear – arrogance, in that we sometimes claim to know the truth already and to have it shut up in a pot, or fear, in that we see quite rightly that the old truth we have loved must die in us so that a new and fuller truth may spring out of it. We must consider this death in a later chapter. It is enough to observe here that love for one another very gently removes these two obstacles. Having climbed off our pedestals and out of our entrenched positions, we find how much more rewarding and delightful it is to learn truth from another than to go on shouting out our own slogans. And though this learning is at the same time painful, I need not be afraid, for the other is not trying to shock me and destroy my faith, but to share with me and to learn from me, so that we may search the height and the depth together as fellow explorers.

The third way in which we experienced the Spirit of truth was as the one who speaks through untrained laymen. This again was what Jesus promised the fishermen from Galilee, who would have to defend themselves before courts of Jewish theologians. 'Do not worry beforehand about what you will say, but when the time comes, say whatever is given you to say; for it will not be you that speak, but the Holy Spirit' (Mark 13:11). We found that laymen and women who had experienced this openness to God and one another, and this exploration of truth together, were able to answer the deepest questions 'graciously and with an astonishing insight'.[2] Graciously, because having learned to be open towards one another, they were now able to be open to their questioner, to listen to them and to treat them as a partner in the search for truth. With an astonishing insight, because the answer they now gave was not something out of a textbook of theology, but a living truth which the Holy Spirit spoke through them. Just as we had discovered that when people begin to love one another with the love of Jesus, they are grasped by a love greater than their own love and when they begin praying together in the name of Jesus they are invaded by a prayer more powerful than their own prayer, so now we were learning a further way of the Spirit's working; when people search together in love and prayer for the truth of Jesus, then they are illuminated by a truth beyond their own reach and grasp of truth.

But our most overwhelming experience of the Spirit of truth was that he led us into *reality*. 'We have seen *reality* break through, like the sun through a fog,' I wrote at the time, 'sweeping away the pretences. People have been set free, to become what they really are.'[3] And this again, of course, was exactly what Jesus promised. When St John is recording the promise of the Spirit of truth, he uses the Greek word *aletheia* which in English we translate *truth* but which might be better translated 'reality' or 'knowledge of reality'.[4] We are to receive the Spirit of reality. The wind of God, who is himself ultimate reality, will blow through us, making us real, blowing away the cobwebs of pretence. Then we shall become the people who we really are, relaxed, free, generous. Then we shall face facts and not be afraid to think things out afresh. Then we shall accept other people as *they* really are, and not try and train them, as circus men train tigers, to jump through a hoop for which their nature never intended them.

The people whom Jesus denounced most forcefully were the unreal people, the hypocrites. He did not condemn the woman taken in adultery, or that nasty little tax collector who had grown rich cheating everybody in Jericho. But he held up to ridicule the unreality of the Pharisees, the men who were outwardly religious, but had no love in their hearts. They took themselves very seriously and they made enormous efforts to evangelise others. But Our Lord's comment upon them was, 'Alas for you, lawyers and Pharisees, hypocrites! You travel over sea and land to win one convert, and when you have won him you make him twice as fit for hell as you are yourselves' (Matthew 23:15). This is false religion, or religiosity. (I can only describe it because I recognise it in myself. Again, this criticism is not directed at anyone else.)

When the Spirit of reality began to blow through the diocese, he made religiosity look ridiculous. For he is like laughter. He says very tenderly, 'Try not to take yourselves so seriously.' This hurts at first – it is a rather unexpected thing for God to say. But as you get used to it, and relax, and become yourself, then Our Lord the Spirit of reality says again, 'Let me come and be in you your true self. For what you really are is a person of love and prayer. You have it in you to be a son or daughter of God, full of the generous self-giving love of Jesus, and gloriously free because you are utterly at his disposal.' And then with a great gust of laughter the Holy Spirit of reality cries out, 'And let other people be *themselves*.'

---

1   See chapter 3 and Acts 4:13.
2   See chapter 3.
3   See end of chapter 7.
4   C.H. Dodd, *The Interpretation of the Fourth Gospel*, p177.

Chapter 11

The New Evangelism

EVANGELISM is the proclaiming of good news about Jesus.

Jesu, my Master and my God,
Assist me to proclaim
And spread through all the earth abroad
The wonders of thy name.

But it is not instructing people about something which I know and they don't. It is rather helping them to discover what they already know and to become what already they really are. The first principle of evangelism must be that the Spirit of truth is already within the person whom I am approaching as an evangelist. That person and I are going to discover the truth together. We are colleagues on a journey of exploration and during this exploration I am going to learn from them as much as they learn from me, and together we are going to discover something which neither of us could discover by ourselves.

So evangelism is a costly adventure for the evangelist, for it involves a sort of little death. The evangelist will have to emerge from the encounter a changed person. He or she will have to admit that what they have so far grasped of the truth has been inadequate. I sometimes say that my job as a Diocesan Missioner is to stop missions, by which I mean stop Christians telling those whom they class as non-Christians the truths which they think they have grasped hold of and shut up in a pot. What in fact we have got to do is to put ourselves together at the disposal of God, so that we are no longer 'us' and 'them', but a company who may be grasped together by the Spirit of truth.

In chapter 2 we foresaw that all our preparations for the consecration of our Cathedral and ourselves would only bring us to a starting point. But a starting point towards what?

Now the answer has become clear – towards evangelism. The Holy Spirit of truth has been teaching us the new way of evangelism, or perhaps it would be better to say recalling us to the way of evangelism as taught by Jesus. This is, of course, exactly what Jesus told us to expect. 'The Holy Spirit, whom the Father will send in my name, will teach you everything, and will call to mind all that I have told you' (John 14:26).

This way of evangelism is set out in St Luke, chapter 10, when Our Lord is sending out the Seventy. It demands first of all that the evangelists *love one another*. They are sent two by two, because it is where two or three go together in the name of Jesus that his power will leap out of the midst. Secondly, they are commanded to *pray*. They must put themselves at the disposal of the Lord of the harvest, whose crop they are going to reap.

Now comes one of the most encouraging verses in the New Testament: 'I am sending you like lambs among wolves.' Picture that scene in your imagination – the fleecy, juicy lamb trembling in the middle of a pack of wolves: they are closing in on him; their jowls are dripping saliva in anticipation of the delicious moment when fangs will close in on flesh and drip with blood. 'That is how evangelists are to go,' said Jesus, '*to be torn in pieces.*' This is most encouraging because we generally imagine that evangelists go out as wolves among lambs, strong men, well-equipped, to answer every question and to rend in pieces every adversary. Knowing that we are not such supermen, we suppose 'evangelism is not for me'. But Jesus told the Seventy exactly the opposite: they were to go out to be torn in pieces and they were to carry no equipment with them. This is something any fool can do.

Their method was to be *love*. They were to speak to people in an ordinary, friendly way, saying 'Peace be to this house' (the equivalent to our 'Good Evening'). They were to *accept hospitality*. Jesus says this twice, so that there can be no doubt about it. They are to 'stay in one house, sharing their food and drink', not being in a hurry, and accepting people as they are. 'Do not move from house to house ... eat the food provided for you.' They will listen and care about the other and their job; they will come to understand them; they will tell them in return about themselves; they will not be ashamed to let them see their need, and they will gratefully accept what they have to give.

Then, when the tensions are relaxed, their hosts will begin to reveal to them the needs and troubles of their household, for they will recognise in them a compassion and an authority which calls out an answering spirit of trust. And now the next stage becomes possible. Jesus says, 'Heal the sick there.' This may mean the sick in mind or in body; it may involve a quarrel that has to be reconciled or a deep-seated fear that has to be faced and cast out. But now the evangelists and their hosts have become a company of friends, conscious together of their need, ready to turn to God and be invaded by the power of his living presence.

Only then is the evangelist commanded to preach. Then they must say 'the kingdom of God has come close to you', for now they are explaining the secret of something which has actually happened. They are proclaiming the good news about Jesus.

This new way of evangelism was first pointed out to me by a

girl from Angola in Africa. Her name was Maria, and she was always laughing. One day we were discussing evangelism and talking about pamphlets, missions, campaigns. After a while somebody turned to Maria. 'What do you do in your church, Maria?' 'In my church,' said Maria, after a moment's thought, 'we don't give pamphlets to people or have missions. We just send one or two Christian families to live in a village, and when people see what Christians are like, then they want to be Christians themselves.'

My eyes were further opened by observing what actually happens when 'pamphlets, missions, campaigns' take place. The hope behind so many of these missions was to 'get more people into the church'. I say *was*, because I believe that during the last few years God has shown us that this kind of spiritual imperialism is not according to his will though we do it with the best intentions. The uncomfortable fact about the mission aimed to 'get more people into the church' was that by and large it did not succeed. After a year of prayer and preparation, after an immense amount of sacrificial work, after a series of gospel sermons preached by a first-class preacher who was on fire with the truth of their message, there were often no more people in the church after a 'mission' than there had been before. In some cases I know there were actually fewer. It was like Han Andersen's fairy story about the emperor's clothes. The emperor believed so firmly that he had put on a beautiful new suit that everybody else pretended to believe so too, and as he walked by in his vest and pants they applauded and exclaimed how beautiful his new suit was. Finally a child, in all innocence, remarked that the emperor had nothing on.

The stark truth about 'the mission' was usually that the size of the church congregation had not increased. (Everybody will know an exception, but this remains overwhelmingly true.) Are we to believe, then, that God had not blessed our efforts and that all our prayers and preparation and preaching had been in vain?

Nobody who has taken part in such a mission could possibly say so. But if they are honest, what they would have to say is, 'I entered this campaign hoping God would convert Mrs Jones, and he has converted me.' What always comes out of a mission (and I cannot remember one exception to this rule) is that church members who are involved in running it are themselves brought to a deeper experience of Christian life. They are welded into a company of people between whom the barriers are down and who have begun to love one another with the love of Jesus. They are forced into prayer together by the enormity of the task they have undertaken and their own inability to carry it out. Then, as surely as day follows night, there comes the fire and the wind and the flowing water, the Spirit of love and prayer and reality. There is a light in their eyes and a song in their hearts. I have seen it again and again.

It is as though God said, 'Do you really want to convert Mrs Jones?' 'Yes, Lord.' 'But wait a moment, do you *really* want to? For the condition is that I must first convert *you*.'

This is the pattern which the Coventry story unfolds. It is the pattern of a stone falling into the middle of a pond, and the ripples spreading outwards. The first ripple was the clergy. They saw from the beginning, with a clear-sighted humility, that they themselves must first be more deeply consecrated before they could expect anyone else to be. I wish all those who abuse the parish clergy could take note of that. We are attacked for not being supermen, but this is not what God wants us to be. He wants us only to know our need of him and to be always ready to be torn to pieces. Then his power can leap out of us and help many people. In the hour of opportunity the clergy of the Coventry Diocese did not fail their vocation, but they followed the example of Jesus who 'did not think to snatch at equality with God, but made himself nothing … and humbled himself' (Philippians 2:8). They learnt to love and to pray at a deeper level, and a new power broke out of them because they became more nearly a fellowship of the Holy Spirit. Then the second ripple could follow, and after that the third and the fourth, as the clergy–laity groups, the parishes, and finally, the whole diocese was grasped by the Spirit of love and prayer and reality.

Now must follow the fifth ripple, which is Christian unity between the denominations. Perhaps what we have learnt and can usefully tell others is not to get bogged down in abstract discussions about truth. If we can only have the courage to love one another with the love of Jesus and to pray together in the name of Jesus, then the Spirit of truth himself will spring out of our midst, and guide us into all truth.

And in all this we are learning the way of evangelism.

First, that we have got to *be* the thing which we proclaim. 'When people see what Christians are like,' said Maria, 'then they want to be Christians themselves.' We have got to *be* the loving community in which they are confronted by the compassion of Jesus, and the praying community in which they are confronted by the authority of Jesus, a Church which makes them exclaim in astonishment, 'See how these Christians love one another.' They must recognise a new kind of social life in which forgiveness operates, a life more real, natural, rich, happy and full-blooded than that which they see in the rest of humanity. This is the new life which we call the Holy Spirit. It is infectious. It is like the leaven in a loaf of bread, permeating the whole, taking the stodginess out of it, causing it to rise and be light and be itself. It is like fire which must spread, like a river which must overflow.

So, secondly, evangelism is not something into which the clergy have to flog unwilling laity, whipping and goading them. Evangelism is the inevitable outpouring of love. If the fire of love is burning in a church that church cannot help evangelising, and if the fire is not burning, then all its evangelistic effort is not only useless, but I believe positively satanic. Like the Pharisees, we travel over land and sea to win one convert, but when we have won him we make him twice as fit for hell as we are ourselves. For instead of setting him free in the fellowship of the Holy Spirit, where he may become gloriously himself, we imprison him in an unloving ecclesiastical system.

But, thirdly, there is a *method* of evangelism. We must not only approach other people with the love of God in our hearts, but we must know how to express it. I heard recently of a schoolteacher who was teaching the children Religious Knowledge. 'What did Jesus come into the world for?' he asked. There was no answer. 'What did he come for?' shouted the exasperated teacher. Still no answer. 'LOVE' he roared at them, striding around the classroom, hitting each child over the head, 'LOVE! LOVE! LOVE!'

This might be justified as a way of teaching Religious Knowledge, but the Christian method of proclaiming love must be by loving. It begins with listening rather than with talking, with being alongside people, coming to understand them, accepting them just as they are, learning from them. All this must be done without any ulterior motive. We are not laying a crafty trap into which we hope they will walk, we are not trying to 'get them to church', we do not approach them as though we alone have the truth, and want to thrust it down their throats like an antibiotic capsule to cure them from sin. Rather, we approach because in them lies a part of God's truth which we need to know ourselves; because above all, we really do love them, and it is fun to talk with them. If we don't love them, then *wait*, as Jesus told his disciples to wait until the Spirit of love had been given to them. 'You must wait,' he said, 'for the promise made by my Father, about which you have heard me speak … you will be baptised with the Holy Spirit, and within the next few days' (Acts 1:4–5).

Love listens, partly for the fun of it, but partly also because it wants to help and this involves making an accurate and unsentimental assessment of others' needs. We must come to under-stand not only their personal problems, but also the social condi-tions by which they are prevented from being themselves. This may lead us into problems of town planning, transport, educa-tion, freedom from hunger, and in the end, politics. But in all this we are only following the example of Jesus himself who, before he preached, spent thirty years listening and learning and being involved in the commercial life of his own day, and who when he did finally embark on his 'ministry', showed himself to be equally concerned with people's bodies as with their souls.

Love listens, love helps, but in the end love tells the secret. It would be silly to say that talking and preaching play no part in evangelism. Of course they do, only it is the *last* part. All I plead is that we should not talk too much and too soon. A young man told me the other day that he felt an antipathy to the clergy because they are people who talk about love. This is a healthy antipathy, for the love of God is something that we must first *be*, and then *do*, before we can talk about it. The love of God is the Holy Spirit welling up from within us, and he it is who is the real evange-list. He speaks through what Christians are, and through what Christians do, and he alone has the power to lead men and women to Jesus. But he speaks to and leads these men and women from *within* themselves; it is not just that they see Jesus externally in his Christians and hear Jesus speaking to them and calling them from over there in his Church. The call sounds in their own hearts, because the Christians have come and stood alongside them and become utterly identified with them; they have not loved them in any patronising and superior way, but have become one company with them, out of which can spring the Spirit of reality, invading 'believers' and 'unbelievers' with new truth.

This is evangelism, the Spirit of reality speaking in a person's heart; it is not something we can engineer, but something that will happen in God's own time, if we love and pray deeply enough. Then is the moment for talking and for preaching, for then we can point them to Jesus, in whom the secret of what they have already experienced is revealed for those who have eyes to see and ears to hear. Preaching is effective in proportion as the listener is already converted. For those who are fast asleep to the reality of God, preaching is just an ineffective bore; for those who are slumbering lightly and dreaming, it may be like the alarm clock which becomes part of the dream and wakes us to the morning; but for those who are already awake, it can be truth sounding to truth in the depths of their being. Then a Christian may talk about love, and bring a man or woman to Jesus, where they will discover what they already know and become what they truly are.

This is the aim of the operation which we call evangelism, not that everybody should come to church, but that all should be set free to praise God by being what they really are. This is the terribly hard re-adjustment we Christians have got to make. We have to give up all attempts to dominate other people and work only to set them free, so that the Holy Spirit of reality may grasp hold of them, and do with them whatever he wishes. Once we have made the re-adjustment in our own thinking, we are aware of an immense sense of relief and relaxation of tension. Then we can help others to relax. Instead of screwing up, our job is unscrewing, because the Holy Spirit is shut up inside, like fire that cannot burn brightly when it has not enough air, like water in a great reservoir that cannot flow into people's houses when all the sluice gates, stopcocks and taps are closed.

But as each woman and man is set free by love, so it happens that they praise God just by being themselves. I saw this truth one March morning when I was driving along a country lane and two hares sprang across the road in front of my car. Running, leaping, courting, just by being perfectly themselves, they revealed the swiftness, the fertility, the exuberance of God. 'O all ye hares, bless ye the Lord, praise him and magnify him for ever.'

So with the human race. It is God's plan and secret purpose that by the love of Jesus we should be set free, each to be ourselves, and to become a song of praise in every fibre of our being. For as when the sun shines on a garden, the flowers open to reveal marvels of colour and design, and from the heart of each there rises a scent, so men, women and children, as they turn to the love of God that shines in the face of Jesus Christ, open up to become the glorious people that they really are, and from the heart of each there rises a cry of praise. 'Our Father, which art in heaven, hallowed be thy name.' Each sings that song by being themselves, and they are most perfectly themselves as they sing that song and the harmony of that music is the joy for which the universe was created.

Chapter 12

The New Family

One overwhelming truth emerges from the Coventry story; that the Church is the fellowship of the Holy Spirit or it is nothing. Without the Holy Spirit we cannot love, pray or evangelise in the Christian sense of those words.

Now the Holy Spirit cannot be trapped or held in any kind of ecclesiastical organisation, but we have been shown that there are conditions for his coming, and that we could at least offer him the kind of organisation through which he most easily operates. The conditions are compassion, and waiting together upon God in prayer; and something could be done to reorganise ourselves so as to give these two qualities more elbow room.

At present they are in short supply and are not obviously the hallmarks of the Church. The ordinary sinner expects the Church to condemn rather than to have compassion on them and the image of the Church in their mind is certainly not of a company of people waiting upon God in prayer, but rather of a lone vicar tearing round the parish in a fury of activity.

Our lack of compassion is very serious and un-Christlike. The day before writing this chapter I had to speak in Coventry Cathedral in the middle of a big scandal which had rocked the country and which by the time these words are read will, I hope, have been forgotten. I began by saying, 'The time has come for the Church to speak out.' There were 2,000 people sitting there, and every one of them expected me to proceed to a condemnation of vice, for that is what the Church is expected to do when she 'speaks out'. When I went on, 'This is what the Church says: "Be compassionate, as your Father is compassionate. Judge not, that you be not judged. Condemn not that you be not condemned."', everyone was astonished. Similarly, Bishops are expected to condemn deviance, but not to go and enjoy the company of those who seem to be beyond the social pale. This would be shocking to public opinion, as it was shocking when Jesus went and enjoyed the company of tax collectors. By condemning sin but failing in compassion to sinners we are in fact living BC rather than AD, denying the revolution which Jesus inaugurated and blocking up the fountain of healing which he opened when he said to the woman taken in adultery, 'Has no one condemned you? … No more do I. You may go, do not sin again.' I am convinced that the reason we fail to show Christ's compassion outside the Church is because we have first failed to obey his New Commandment inside and that part of the reason we fail inside is because our ecclesiastical set-up makes Christlike love difficult.

The same is true about 'waiting together upon God in prayer'. Here again our failure is very serious. It results in platitudinous preaching, lack of creative leadership, overworked and exhausted priests, and a laity frustrated because they are given no real responsibility. Partly to blame for this is again our ecclesiastical set-up.

I refer in particular to parishes, priests and Prayer Book, the three glories of the Church of England.

There is no community richer in human relations than a little English parish where people care for one another and belong together round a village church. At the heart of this community is the vicar, praying for everyone in the village by name, and understanding and loving each one. On Sunday the family gathers together to praise God through the words of the Prayer Book, to hear the Bible read and to receive the sacraments, to be caught up by the well-loved cadences and the rhythm of the church's year into a worship that does not depend upon the mood of the worshippers and is not invalidated by the unworthiness of the priest. This system of parish, priest and Prayer Book has been transplanted to the cities and has taken root with partial success even in modern housing estates. I personally have been nurtured in it, and love it passionately. But I believe that these things, as well as being the great strength of the Church of England, are also its fatal weaknesses; at one and the same time they are its glory, and the tomb in which it is imprisoned, and from which it must break out if it is to live. Many have broken out in the last four centuries, of whom the most obvious examples already mentioned in this book are the Quakers and the Methodists. The exciting thing about the Coventry story is that here the same breakout is happening under the leadership of a Bishop, and that this time the break*out* need not be a break*away*, but rather a rebirth of the full catholic tradition in contemporary form.

First, we must break out of the rigidity of the parish system, for in the twentieth century the parish is both too large and too small. It is too large, as we have already seen, because many a loyal Anglican may worship all their life in the parish church but never become deeply involved with their fellow Christians. For this each needs to belong to a smaller group of not more than twelve people who have the courage to be open to one another, and together open to God. Enough has been said about this already, and descriptions given of small groups at work. But now we must emphasise that the parish is also too small. This is no longer the age of the footpath winding over the fields to the next hamlet. It is the age of motorways and air travel and of satellites, through which in a few years one person may be seen and heard in every corner of the world at a single moment. To think only parochially at such a time is death. We must laugh ourselves out of our jealousy when people in one parish seek help in another. (One of my own parishioners was sick during this past year and after I had failed to help her went to my next door neighbour for spiritual advice, so I know this ecclesiastical jealousy at first hand, and how silly it is, and how it disguises itself under high-sounding names.) We must combine with neighbouring parishes so that we can tackle together in a big, exciting and efficient way such things as youth work and adult lay training. Obviously, some such combination of parishes could be the rural deanery and here we have a piece of machinery to hand which has never yet been properly used, and which may be one of the keys to the revival of church life. Beyond the deanery lies the diocese, and the time is clearly ripe when the diocese must become a living unit. Modern transport makes this for the first time possible, though many dioceses are still far too big for the Bishop to be generally known. One urgent reform now being canvassed is that we should have smaller dioceses, grouped into provinces under Archbishops, so that much of the administration by which a Bishop is now burdened could be done provincially and the Bishops set free to be Fathers in God. At the heart of each diocese the cathedral must come alive as the mother church. To her, parish groups can come and meet one another and find themselves involved in a worship and a vision of the world Church that will kindle their imagination. From her, experts can go to the parishes to encourage and advise in such matters as music and drama, youth work, evangelism, the Church and industry. If the cathedral is really to be the living heart of a diocese then it must be staffed by people in the prime of life and not be used as an honourable retiring place for those whose work is behind them. Honours in the Christian Church seem in any case slightly ridiculous and it might be better if the title of Canon could be reserved for Rural

Deans, who would relinquish it on relinquishing their office, and during the time they held it would be the representative of their part of the diocese on the cathedral chapter. But the most important factor of all is that the cathedral should be the Bishop's church, and that the centre of the whole life of the diocese, and of all love and authority within it, should be seen to be a person – not an administrator in their diocesan house surrounded by typewriters, but a Bishop preaching the word of God and celebrating the Holy Communion in the mother church. And the aim and object of all this softening up of parochial barriers is that we should become a company who love one another, and are together at the disposal of God, so that Our Lord the Holy Spirit of reality may be set free to leap out of our midst on his work of proclaiming Jesus in the secular world.

As with the parish, so with the priest. The time has come for the breakdown of old patterns. All over the world today the laity are discovering who they are and this does not mean that they feel they can do without priests. On the contrary, they need them as never before, to equip them for the stupendous task of being Christ in their generation. But now the relation must be a partnership and at every level the laity must be given and must take their full responsibility in the governing of the Church. At parish level they must share in making policy, hammering it out with the vicar in continuous discussion and prayer. A great deal of work that has been traditionally done by the clergy could well be shared with the laity. For example, in confirmation training, a layperson could prepare a boy or girl to be a Christian at work much better than could most clergy. In large town parishes, lay people can become pastorally responsible for a whole street, making friends and helping people in need and holding discussion meetings in their houses. On the great new housing estates, there might well be appointed paid laymen and women to serve a parish or a group of parishes: a person with business experience, for example, might become the bursar, a retired schoolteacher might become an education or youth officer, a layperson might be employed as full-time secretary. These people should be recognised as having been called by God every bit as much as the clergy and should become part of the staff of the parish as equal partners with them. All this would have the practical effect of setting free the priest to do their own special work of love and prayer, but it might have the even profounder effect of setting free Our Lord the Holy Spirit of love and prayer himself to spring up out of the close fellowship of clergy and laity.

As with the parish and the priest, so with the Prayer Book. Here again the enemy is rigidity and formality. I once talked with some Greek friends about Anglican worship and discovered that, quite frankly, they found us rather funny. 'In our country,' they said, 'we come to church feeling happy. We greet our friends, and we go inside to worship with a sense of freedom. Here you march up to the church looking grim and greeting no-one. You behave inside like soldiers on parade, sitting in rows with your eyes to the front, all getting up and sitting down together at the word of command from your superior officer.' Of course this is partly due to our national temperament, for we like things to be done decently and in order; but my Greek friends were not altogether wrong in laughing at our stiffness, for worship ought to be the moment at which we are most natural and completely ourselves. If we take ourselves very seriously and are afraid to stand up, sit down, sing too loud, or join in the responses lest we make ourselves conspicuous, then we must be making it very difficult indeed for the Holy Spirit to inspire our prayers. It is all too common for a church service to be so tense and unnatural that when the worshippers get home they explode in quarrels with one another, and the effect of this rigidity is particularly devastating upon children. Seeing their parents afraid even to smile when something funny happens, they find it difficult to believe that they are really in the house of a Father who loves them.

We must break out of the stranglehold of the Book of Common Prayer and find place for informality, extemporary prayer, and silence. The Holy Communion at Coventry Cathedral begins with the celebrant saying, 'Good Morning', and inviting the people to sit down while the visitors are welcomed and the congregation told about the service which is to follow. This immediately relaxes tension. Extemporary prayer must find its place, for as Canon Max Warren says, 'One of the surest ways of killing the spirit of inter-cession is to confine one's prayers to generalities.'[1] We all know the electrifying effect in church when the vicar, instead of saying, 'cheer, heal and sanctify the sick', suddenly calls on the people to pray for Tom who is lying unconscious in hospital after a motor accident. And the effect is profoundest of all when they are asked to pray together in silence. Silence is perhaps our greatest need in this busy, noisy century if we are really to pray and our embarrass-ment at silence is a sign of our dis-ease. There is nothing disloyal to the Prayer Book in simply stopping for a moment to 'be still and know that I am God', and in such a moment of corporate silence, people's spirits can be most powerfully invaded by the Spirit of prayer. 'If you ask the Father for anything in my name,' said Jesus, 'he will give it you. So far you have asked nothing in my name. Ask and you will receive, that your joy may be complete' (John 16:22–24). Might he not say it again, with a certain divine exasperation, at the end of many Prayer Book services?

What I have tried to do in this chapter is not to suggest that we abolish parishes, priests and prayer books, but rather to point out that we live in an age when the external patterns of these things are cracking and breaking. This is not a moment to be alarmed, but to rejoice, because the force that is breaking them is the new life of the Holy Spirit welling up from inside, so that out of these things which we have known and loved there is emerging a fuller truth, and they are becoming more perfectly themselves. If we were to cling rigidly to externals at such a moment, and to life as we have known it, we should be like the Pharisees to whom Jesus said, 'Alas, alas, you are like unmarked graves over which men may walk without knowing it', for inside would be death, and everybody who came in contact with us would be contaminated. But as we accept death as part of God's inexorable and loving plan, so new life is born. As the parish ceases to be parochial and becomes a part of a united diocese, so it becomes its true and generous self and reveals the revolutionary secret of Christian compassion. As priests leave behind their ecclesiastical dignity and enter into partnership with the laity, so they become true representatives of Jesus, the great High Priest, and reveal to all believers the secret of their own priesthood. As we relax the formality of Prayer Book worship and allow its majestic sequences to express our common joy, our common love, our common need, so it becomes indeed the Book of Common Prayer, and initiates us into the mystery of praying together in the name of Jesus.

But first there must be a breaking.

---

1   *Danger! People praying*, by M.A.C. Warren, *CMS News Letter*, January 1961.

Chapter 13

The New Covenant

At the end of my garden there is a chestnut tree and every autumn the children gather the conkers and bring them home. They lay them out in rows of glossy and beautiful playthings. But each conker remains sterile unless it has the good fortune to fall into the ground. Then, quite literally, it is broken. Its beauty withers and its glossy coat rots and cracks, as from inside it there pushes out with irresistible force the chestnut tree which that conker really is. It takes root and grows, and as the years pass it bears tens of thousands of conkers that give pleasure to generations of children.

Nature's pattern of breaking, so that new life may spring out, runs also through history and it can be seen in sharpest focus in the pages of the Bible. The Jews had to be broken. They knew themselves to be a chosen people who worshipped the one true God and the worship was centred upon the temple where sacrifices were offered to God in the holy city of Jerusalem. But in 586 BC the temple was destroyed. Jerusalem was reduced to a heap of stones and the Jews were scattered in exile. This seemed to many to be the end of everything they had hoped for, but in fact it was only through being broken that they discovered who they really were and the truth of God was set free to shine out of them. They were chosen, but not, as they had imagined, to rule the world; they were chosen to serve and to heal the world through suffering. God wanted their sacrifices, but not, as they had hitherto understood, the blood of bulls and goats. He wanted the sacrifice of their inmost pride, so that each one of them could say, 'I delight to do thy will, O my God: yea, thy law is within my heart' (Psalm 40:8). All that they had believed up to that point had not been untrue, but it had been inadequate, and now there was a new, richer and fuller truth which was ready to burst out from the ruins of the old. It was a truth about compassion and about prayer, a truth about being open to their fellows and open to God. It was Our Lord the Holy Spirit of truth himself who in that moment of their breaking broke out and 'spoke by the prophets'.

This pattern that runs through nature and history is revealed with an absolute and final clarity in the death of Jesus. He himself likened his own death to the seed falling into the ground so that new life could spring out of it. 'The hour has come,' he said, 'for the Son of Man to be glorified. In truth, in very truth I tell you, a grain of wheat remains a solitary grain unless it falls into the ground and dies; but if it dies it bears a rich harvest' (John 12:23–24). As he died on the cross, there came pouring out of his broken body and soul the new life of the Holy Spirit.

He had been the man of pure compassion, whose hands touched lepers and whose tongue spoke to sinners the healing words of love. But there came the breaking point of compassion, when his hands were nailed to the wood and his tongue was parched and he could no longer act or speak or even feel compassion, but could only cry out in darkness and despair 'My God, my God, why hast thou forsaken me?' Yet out of that darkness there shines a light down the centuries and out of that moment when his compassion was stretched past the utmost point of human endurance till his heart broke, there comes to us and touches us the very compassion of God himself. At that moment we see that we are finally accepted by a love that will never let us go, but that is ready not only to die but even to be made sin for our sake.

So also he had been the man of perfect prayer, whose body had shone with the glory of God as he knelt on the mountain-side in communion with his Father. But there came the breaking point of prayer, the moment on the cross when he saw his life's work ending in disaster, when his friends had deserted him, when his enemies were laughing because after all they were right and he was wrong, and love doesn't work, and God doesn't save. At that moment surely we must believe that the foundations of his faith were shaken, and that he faced the ultimate horror of separation from God, that horror which a mother may know as she watches her child dying, and her cry for help echoes round an empty universe, and prayer dries up within her. But there in the darkness in the soul of Jesus we come face to face with the utter reliability of God, who never for a moment abandoned him. When Jesus could no longer pray we come upon the deepest secret of prayer, that God is upholding us, and that prayer is not in the end something we do, but something God does. It is the Spirit praying within us, and praying most powerfully when we have persevered to the end and passed the limit of our own endurance.

The cross is the breaking point. Out of the broken body of Jesus pours freely the torrent of the Holy Spirit of love and prayer, and the life of the new age begins.

This is the truth which underlies the Coventry story. Our Cathedral was burnt and out of the ruins sprang new life. It had been a glorious piece of mediaeval architecture where the love of God was preached and the praises of God sung. But it had to die before it could bear a rich harvest. Then, as out of the conker from the bottom of the garden, when the glossy shell perished, there pushed the chestnut tree which that conker really was, so out of the destruction of a beautiful Cathedral there has come the opportunity to discover what God really means a Cathedral and a diocese to be in the twentieth century. And as out of the ruins of the temple in Jerusalem long ago there sprang the Holy Spirit of love and prayer, leading the Jews into new and richer truth, so he has come and spoken again, in these last years, to us.

But we have learned that the pattern of this breaking must not only be on our Cathedral, it must be also on ourselves. If we really want to be Christians then we must follow in the way of the cross and this demands of us at every moment *humility*. We must be ready to meet people and learn from them, and we must be ready to be broken by the new truth of God which is coming to birth. This is a painful experience and the story, which this book tells, has been painful to live through. New ideas are terrifying to most of us. Even more terrifying to British people is the demand that we should love one another. (G.K. Chesterton once wrote that the reason so many British people go big game shooting, or risk their lives climbing the Himalayas, is because we are so terrified of our next door neighbour!) But most terrifying of all is that we should put ourselves at the disposal of God so that he may take us and bless us and break us and give us to our fellow men and women.

But this is the truth to which our story has led us. We asked God, 'What does it mean to be a consecrated people?' and he brought us through a new discovery of love and of prayer and of the Holy Spirit back to that moment when Jesus took bread, and blessed it, and broke it, and gave it. This is consecration. This is the moment when Jesus consecrates himself, taking the bread which signifies his own body, holding it up to God in thanksgiving, breaking it, and giving it to his friends. 'Do this in remembrance of me,' he says; and when he commands 'do this', he means first of all that we should re-present his own act of consecration and give thanks for it, as Christians have done ever since at the Eucharist. But this is not all. Do we really want to be a consecrated people? Then we ourselves must be the bread in our Lord's hands and we must pray, 'Lord, take us, bless us, break us, and give us to our fellow men.' During the years that we were preparing for the consecration of our Cathedral we learnt that to be a consecrated people is to be the fellowship of the Holy Spirit, who fills us and overflows into the world. But the condition of receiving this new life is that we walk with Jesus in the way of the cross. We will receive the Holy Spirit if we love with the love of Jesus, and pray in the name of Jesus, to the limit of our endurance and beyond it. This *is* the New Testament.

For the word 'Testament' means covenant and a covenant is an exchange of promises between two parties, as for example between a bridegroom and a bride: 'I take thee,' he says, 'for better or for worse.' 'I take thee,' she replies, 'till death us do part.' That is the marriage covenant. But the New Covenant (or New Testament, as it is more generally known) is an exchange of promises between our bridegroom Jesus Christ and his bride, the Church. This covenant he inaugurated at the last supper, when he gave the cup of wine to his friends.

He was saying grace at the end of the meal, and following the custom of the Jews of his day, he recited a thanksgiving over a special cup of wine. At the end of the thanksgiving this cup was traditionally sipped by whoever had recited the prayer and then handed round to each of those present to sip. During the thanksgiving occur these words, 'We thank thee, O Lord Our God, because thou didst bring us forth from the land of Egypt, and didst deliver us from the house of bondage; as well as for thy covenant, which thou hast sealed in our flesh.'[1] When Jesus had finished that prayer he handed the cup to his friends. So far all had followed the traditional pattern, but now he adds the extraordinary words, 'This cup is the *new* covenant sealed by my blood' (1 Corinthians. 2:25).

At that moment the new age of the world was beginning, the age of the New Covenant. And what were the terms of the covenant? What did each party bind themselves to do?

We can see the answer given by St John, the beloved disciple who was sitting next to Jesus, if we read chapters 13 to 16 of his Gospel. *On our side, we must love one another as Jesus loved us, and pray in his name. On his side, he will send us the Holy Spirit.* The New Commandment and the New Prayer will be met by the New Gift.

Part One of this book ends with the words I wrote myself under the impact of the consecration. 'These are the three who dance together and are one at the heart of the Church – Love, Prayer, the Holy Spirit. All else is secondary.' It is in those chapters of St John's Gospel that the dance is first described. They enter like three ballet dancers, first the New Commandment, then the New Prayer, and finally the New Gift. 'Love one another … ask in my name … I will give you the Spirit of truth.' First one, then another, holds the centre of the stage; they hold hands and dance together; they weave in and out and through one another in intricate patterns. Here is one such moment. 'If you ask anything in my name I will do it. If you love me you will obey my commands; and I will ask the Father, and he will give you another to be your Advocate, who will be with you for ever – the Spirit of truth' (John 14:14–16). Here is another moment, when the original order is reversed, and the promise of the Spirit takes the lead, with the Prayer second and the Command third: 'I appointed you to go on and bear fruit, fruit that shall last; so that the Father may give you all that you ask in my name. This is my commandment to you; love one another' (John 15:16–17).

These three dance together and are one. It is not true to say, 'If we love with the love of Jesus and pray together in his name, *then* he will give us the Holy Spirit.' For how can we love with that love and pray in that name unless the Holy Spirit comes to our help? Nor is it true to say 'Pray first for the Holy Spirit. *Then* you will be filled with the love and the prayer of Jesus,' for the Holy Spirit is only given to those who persevere in love and prayer to the limit of their endurance and beyond it.

These three dance together and are one, and that one is Jesus Christ. And he gives us all three at once as he gives us himself, his crucified body and his risen life. 'For their sakes I now consecrate myself, that they too may be consecrated by the truth' (John 17:19).

1   Gregory Dix: *The Shape of the Liturgy*, p52f.

+ Epilogue

Perspective

WHEN THE
COMFORTER IS COME +
EVEN THE SPIRIT OF TRUTH
+ YE ALSO SHALL
BEAR WITNESS

Chapter 14

The New Age

Imagine that it is your duty to keep a diary of the world from the day of its formation until now, writing one page for every thousand years.

For the first milliards of years there would have been little activity to record. The world lay in silence, for as yet there were no dogs to bark or even leaves to rustle. There were only rocks, and the occasional rumble of a volcano, and the sound of the wind blowing across the empty spaces of the sea in which no life stirred.

But perhaps you would have sensed, in the silence, a growing expectancy, as though something was just about to happen. You would have noticed preliminary stirrings; and then one day, somewhere, you observed and recorded the first cell. Molecules, grouped and combined in a certain way round a nucleus, had come alive. A new era had started, the era of LIFE.

Now the face of the earth was changing as the cells multiplied and evolved. First the oceans teemed with life, with seaweeds and sponges, crabs and fishes. Then it emerged on to the dry land, till the bare rocks were covered with grass and flowers and trees. Reptiles crawled, birds flew, creatures hopped and ran. Everywhere was colour and sound and movement. You watched and recorded for about a thousand million years, as gigantic dinosaurs evolved and became extinct, and life pressed on towards yet more perfect expressions of itself. And then you noticed a creature developing a large head, and within that head a great brain. For a while you could not be certain whether or not they were different in any important sense but one day quite recently, only about half a million years ago, you wrote in your diary that the first human had begun to think. A new era had started, the era of HOMO SAPIENS.

What makes human beings different is that they are 'self-conscious'. Each one can say, 'I am'. They are the active centres of their own existence, with the power to choose and plan and make jokes. Cows grazing in a field are not in this sense self-conscious, and they cannot choose. They just go where the grass is greenest or where they are driven (which is why one small child of *Homo sapiens* can drive a whole herd of cows). Homo sapiens has again changed the face of the earth; we have cleared jungles and swamps, built cities, and irrigated deserts. We have dug mines and crossed the sea and now at last flown off into space.

But with all our marvellous brains we have a fatal flaw. Human beings' very self-consciousness, which gives us the power to choose and invent and write poetry, at the same time makes it difficult for us to live at peace with our neighbour. Our greatest glory is at the same time our fatal weakness. Being self-conscious, we are also self-centred. When you want one thing and I want another, and we both want them badly enough, then in the last resort we clash. Friends quarrel, homes break up, and countries go to war. Consequently, we have arrived at the fantastic situation when Homo sapiens with their great brains are threatening to commit suicide. Just at the very moment when the world is becoming so small that we can fly to any part of it in a few hours, when before long, using satellites, a pianist could appear simultaneously and play the same bit of music in every house all over the world, or a clown set the whole human race laughing by a single gesture, just at the moment when we might become one family, we are threatening to blow ourselves and all life off the face of the earth.

But now comes the good news. Yesterday, just in the nick of time, a new era started, the era of JESUS CHRIST.

I say *yesterday*, because if you had been keeping that diary and had written one page for every thousand years, though your volumes would by now require about two miles of library shelf to accommodate them, you would only have to pick up the last volume and turn back one page to read the story of Jesus.

Jesus was 'Homo sapiens' in every particular except the all-important one, that he was not self-centred. He was highly self-conscious, having this distinctive feature of Homo sapiens to a marked degree, so that he not only said, 'I am' but reiterated it and based his teaching upon it ('I am the bread of life … I am the light of the world … I am the door of the sheep … I am the good shepherd … I am the resurrection and the life … I am the true vine … I am the way, the truth and the life'). But within this heightened self-consciousness he acknowledged the centre of his existence to be not himself, but God his Father. He put himself absolutely at the disposal of God in prayer, and at the same time lived a life of utter compassion towards his fellows. In him there appeared a new kind of life called HOLY SPIRIT. There had been preliminary manifestations of Holy Spirit before his time, but as with the first cell and the first Homo sapiens, so now with Jesus; others had felt the stirrings of the new life, but in Jesus it had fully arrived. The Holy Spirit 'spoke by the prophets' and five hundred years before Jesus great men like Confucius, Isaiah and Socrates were teaching about love and prayer. But Jesus actually *was* what they had taught; he was himself 'conceived by the Holy Ghost', the man of love and prayer and reality, the only-begotten son of God.

He ended his life with a reckless act of complete compassion and obedience, by which this new life was set free to be given to his friends. Raised from the dead, he breathed upon them and said, 'Receive the Holy Spirit.'

Now was beginning that new age of the world which he had called the kingdom of God and which had been preparing for millions of years from before the creation of the world. This is a moment as startlingly new and decisive as the creation of the first cell, for now the promise of Jesus is being realised: 'I have come that men may have life, and may have it in all its fullness' (John 10:10). These friends of his are to be centred no longer upon themselves, but upon him. His love and authority have roused up in each one individually an answering faith, and in that faith they can receive his life into their own and become capable of obeying his New Commandment, that 'as I have loved you, so you are to love one another'. So there springs into existence a new kind of fellowship. As molecules centred round a nucleus had come alive, so those first Christians centred round Jesus came alive together with Holy Spirit. They became who they really were and what the human race really is. They were grasped by a new quality of compassion and prayer and reality which, in the words of their own contemporaries, turned the world upside down.

This new age only began yesterday, and like the life of the cell so the life of the first Christian company has reproduced itself in an infinite and beautiful variety. We can take courage at the astonishing speed with which it has spread into every corner of the world, for the kingdom is still less than two days old, and we ourselves are almost the first Christians. Sometimes we are depressed by the Church because it seems so unlike the fellowship of the Holy Spirit, so rigid and lacking in compassion, so busy and empty of prayer, so out of touch with reality, both with the reality of men and women and the reality of God. But the new life of the Holy Spirit is revolutionary, and we ought not to be surprised if it is taking Homo sapiens in general, and the followers of Jesus in particular, a little time to adjust ourselves to the idea of it. It is not easy for us to become humble and to admit that at the very centre of ourselves is a power of love greater than ourselves, by whom we must be grasped and invaded if we are to become the people who we really are. It is harder still for us to drop our defences and to expose ourselves daily to this love of God. It is even more difficult to open ourselves in compassion to the needs of our fellows. It is most difficult and painful of all to admit how much we need their compassion and how impoverished we are for lack of the truth which they understand.

If fact it is impossible. It is to be broken. It is death. We cling desperately to familiar patterns and inadequate truths, but new life is bursting out from within, Our Lord the Spirit of truth himself. We see him everywhere in our generation, for his time is ripe, and to block his course and to deny his reality is the ultimate blasphemy for which Jesus warned us there was no forgiveness (Mark 3:27). God is breaking us, so that he may give us to our fellow men and women. We are lucky to be alive at such a moment.